Praise for

Think Like a Brand.
Act Like a Startup.

"A fascinating blend of insights and actionable strategies. Whether you're an aspiring founder or leading innovation for an established brand, this book is your go-to for building a high-growth venture."

—**Keith Ferrazzi,** #1 *New York Times* best-selling author

"As we look at what will define the next wave of innovation, we see an acute need to crack the code on startup-enterprise collaboration. Lauren Perkins breaks down the roles of enterprises and startups, shedding light on a new approach for the next generation of founders."

—**Cait Brumme,** CEO, MassChallenge

"In a world that demands more of business leaders at every turn, Lauren Perkins breaks down the traditional superpowers of enterprises and startups, offering growth-oriented leaders a concrete and actionable path for blending stability with agility to create lasting impact and personally sustainable success."

—**Alex Johnston,** best-selling author, *Money with Meaning*

"For any innovative leader wanting to flip uncertainty into opportunity, Lauren Perkins's new book is a game-changer!"

—**James Laughlin,** host, *Lead On Purpose* podcast

Drive Growth and Innovation by
Balancing Stability and Agility.

Think Like a Brand.

Act Like a Startup.

Lauren Perkins

AN INC.
ORIGINAL

An Inc. Original
New York, New York
www.anincoriginal.com

This work is being published under the An Inc. Original imprint by an exclusive arrangement with Inc. Magazine. Inc. Magazine and the Inc. logo are registered trademarks of Mansueto Ventures, LLC. The An Inc. Original logo is a wholly owned trademark of Mansueto Ventures, LLC.

Think Like a Brand. Act Like a Startup. and affiliated entities are trademarks of Lauren Perkins.

Distributed by River Grove Books

Design and composition by Greenleaf Book Group
Cover design by Anna Lassen & Rafaela Valencia-Dongo

Publisher's Cataloging-in-Publication data is available.

Print ISBN: 978-1-63909-036-5

eBook ISBN: 978-1-63909-037-2

First Edition

To every innovator, creator, and entrepreneur
out there designing the future,

and to Hailey and Leah, who embody fearless,
playful, and messy experimentation

Contents

Acknowledgments

This book has been quite a journey.

I'll start at the beginning. My mother was a corporate communications director and a gifted visual artist. She is still one of the most creative people I've ever met. She taught me to get my point across effectively while staying alive in the moment. My father studied mathematics and spent his career as a data engineer. Without consciously setting out to do so, he taught me the importance of data, benchmarking, and continuous improvement while taking a grounded, analytical approach to every challenge, starting with my early days as a competitive swimmer.

Between them, they taught me both creative and data-driven approaches to problem-solving. They also gave me a deep appreciation for the need for each approach, individually and used together. I owe them everything, including my ability to come up with data-driven and creative solutions to problems in business and life. Thanks, Mom! Thanks, Dad!

Another lesson in the importance of clear communication came when I worked for our local newspaper in high school. That job taught me how to do research to uncover facts, trends, insights, user needs, etc. Most importantly, it showed me how to get and keep people's attention with the ability to craft a compelling story with a hook based on said uncovered info.

My entire childhood was a blend of communication, artistry, data, process, and stats. Believe it or not, it was a lot of fun! Did I really have any choice but to plunge into entrepreneurship and innovation?

Bringing this book to life has been a team effort! From Barbara, my longtime collaborator and co-conspirator, to all the beautiful GEMS (Global Executive Masters of Science) at Parsons who read the early iterations and provided necessary feedback and inspiration for the design thinking applied throughout this book. From Priti, who worked so diligently early on to help me craft the path for the manuscript's first iteration, to the incredible strategic designers Anna and Rafaela, who have joined me in this creative journey and provided invaluable insights and much-needed humor in the long stretches. Thank you to my former Microsoft right hand and protégé, Paulina, who I'm so proud took all the learnings and insights into her transition to VC (Venture Capital), and who read, re-read, and re-re-read the manuscript enough times to know it by heart. And for the last-minute assist in the final stretch of proofing and production from my friend Lara at Google—who said competing tech ventures can't play nice? This book would not have been possible without the tireless efforts of my editors, Jen, Nathan, and the rest of the team—you guys rock! A huge thank you to my first editor, Mike, for taking a chance on me.

Finally, a big thank you to all the fellow entrepreneurs, corporate innovators, team leaders, creatives, and operators I've crossed paths with over the years. To the teams and leaders at Columbia

University, General Assembly, Parsons, Startup Weekend, and Microsoft for Startups: thank you for your faith, support, and for the experiences that have helped shape my career. And a special thank you to the thousands of startup founders whom I've had the opportunity to teach and share my experiences with across the world, and who served as willing test subjects for the material in this book—I learned valuable lessons from each and every one of you. I hope this book makes you proud.

Preface

I've taken a company from imminent bankruptcy to acquisition. I've scaled a brick-and-mortar startup from $1.5 million to $10 million in two years without fundraising. I've rescued a founder from walking away from a chaotic yet profitable startup. I wish I could say that I exaggerated the direness of the situations of these three startups or that those situations only play out occasionally. The truth is that, whether they end in triumph, extinction, or a slow slide into irrelevance, these scenarios have played out countless times for many founders.

What keeps founders up at night? What do they do when a key customer or revenue stream disappears seemingly overnight, and they wake up feeling hopeless? This sleepless founder will send out an SOS text to a fixer: *I'm out of time/money/runway/sanity! I don't know what to do! I need help ASAP!*

I know this because I have been one of those fixers. Founders call me when sh*t is hitting the fan, they've hit an inflection point, or they're growing out of control. Many I've worked with explicitly ask me for a Hail Mary to turn a company around or to fix the growth engine so a venture can scale up. What I bring to the table—what I use to turn companies around from behind the scenes—are my journalistic roots, my marketing expertise, my experience as a founder, my discipline as a triathlete, and the principles outlined in this book.

I never set out to be a struggling founder's midnight fixer. In an ideal world, I'd spend most of my time advising, teaching, and writing books like this one. It's my goal that after reading this book, you will never need to text me or anyone else that SOS. I'm laying out my operational-growth framework so that you can use my fifteen years of experience as a startup founder and CMO turned corporate innovator and portfolio manager to build your business the right way—or at least make better mistakes and save yourself the lost runway, capital, and frustration of the last generation of startup founders.

I once chatted with the director of operations at a thriving startup whose founder was eager to bring me on as their founding Chief Marketing Officer (CMO). This ops lead was not having it, though. She insisted, "You're the CMO we'll hire in three years if we fuck up!" As complimentary as that was, I had to ask her, "What if this time you built and firetested the foundation properly from the beginning? How might that positively change your job, the culture, the experience for your customers and employees, and the value of the company? Might all the stakeholders enjoy less struggle?"

This startup operator had gotten so used to the fire drills, the hustle, and grinding it out that she hadn't thought there was another way—a better, more sustainable way to de-risk building and scaling a startup. You might be thinking, *Maybe they couldn't afford you!* That wasn't it, either. They had plenty of cash from a past exit and strong cash flow but no idea how to invest it wisely.

This book is for her. And for you. While there is no magic pill, let's give you a leg up from the start, shall we?

Introduction

The purpose of a business is
to create and keep a customer.

— Peter Drucker

Established brands are the behemoths of the business world. They have a strong customer base and have built a stable foundation for continued growth. At the same time, they're ungainly and hard to steer, and their inherent bureaucracy and risk avoidance make innovation a constant challenge, especially in the face of unexpected crises. In contrast, startups move quickly, turn on a dime, and can follow, anticipate, or create markets for new products and revenue streams. Their agility comes at a price, though: They are fragile, unstable, and exist in constant uncertainty until their idea either takes hold . . . or doesn't.

I've worked with and led both large, established brands and startups—including my own. Each has benefits and drawbacks, but by identifying and combining the best aspects of both, an innovator can create stable growth, support innovation, and minimize risks. Thinking like a brand allows startups to plan better and create the stable base of a corporation. Acting like a startup allows established companies to use their earned market power to embrace innovation and stay competitive. Either type of company can thrive in a world of constant change if they think like a brand and act like a startup.

Think Like a Brand.

A brand is a set of expectations, experiences, values, and relationships that, when taken together, accounts for a consumer's perception of a product or service and ultimately drives their selection of one product or service over another. The best brands do an excellent job of tapping into the emotions, desires, and dreams of their customers. They're expert storytellers and content creators. When they strike the right balance, their advertising and marketing establish a strong bond of loyalty with their customers by building a real human connection. What's more, established brands usually develop long-term strategies and processes to maintain that loyalty, targeting the big picture and tying them to quarterly earnings results. There are three key attributes to thinking like a brand:

Clarity

Brands are driven by clarity. When the brand identity clearly shows who the company is and who it isn't, it acts as a magnet for customers who really see the value in the company's solution while deflecting low-margin customers.

Identity

An established brand has a human-like identity that resonates deeply with its customers and taps into their aspirations to evolve ahead of those customers to keep the brand relevant. This is portrayed to its audience through tailored experiences and polished storytelling.

Stability

Effective brands have sticking power and longevity—which results in healthy profit margins—and strong customer lifetime value metrics that allow thriving brands to successfully bring new iterations or products to market regularly.

Brands that drive demand start with consumer insights, needs, pain points, and opportunities and then determine how to best deliver value to that customer in a unique way that others can't. They create clarity and a sense of identity for their customers and for their people. This clarity not only drives demand and relevance but also influences decision-making for customers and employees alike. When you think in terms of building a brand rather than a company, it shifts your focus to long-term customer impact.

The flip side of this is that brands can struggle with change and crisis. Although the stability of brands provides a solid foundation to assess the right opportunity to engage customers and add value, focusing on those long-term strategies creates a material risk that the company will lack the responsiveness and agility to adjust to changing circumstances. Many legacy companies worry that innovative products or services will cannibalize existing lines of business or their stock price. In addition, brands can be hamstrung by regulatory environments, existing contractual obligations, and, of course, shareholder earning expectations.

Despite these difficulties, becoming a brand is crucial to the long-term success of a company. Cultivating a brand to match or even exceed the market size creates lifelong customers and fans. It goes beyond name recognition and becomes part of the identity of the consumer. Like a sports team, the brand's core customers don't just buy the product; they buy T-shirts and hats with the product's name on them. They root for the brand and support it when they're needed. They become part of the brand in a way that is crucial to its success.

Act Like a Startup.

Being a big company with a long history of success does not secure you a place in customers' hearts and minds in the present, let alone in the future. There are quite a few well-known examples of previously successful companies that failed to adapt and lost their market share to newer evolutions of their business (Kodak and Nokia spring to mind). Entrepreneurship culture brings a bold and lean aspect to business. Startups that grew from two people in a basement to multibillion-dollar corporations are surpassing traditional companies on any number of core business and customer metrics (see Meta, formerly Facebook, Uber, and Zoom).

Startups live with extreme uncertainty. They offer products or services that have not yet proven their value in the market. They also share a few other characteristics:

Curiosity

The most successful startups embrace curiosity. They constantly challenge conventional wisdom and ask why, what if, and why not.

They focus on fresh possibilities rather than on what already is. Startups look to the horizon, not at their feet.

Constraints

Whether it be time, money, capital, or some combination of the three, constraints are guardrails that drive a startup's focus and impact. Constraints allow new possibilities to emerge along with a focus only on what generates value.

Agility

Startups use speed to their advantage and operate with a sense of urgency. In contrast to big companies, startups are not slowed down by inflexible policies or processes. Their agility allows them to take advantage of opportunities as they appear.

Startups can improve performance through iteration. They are great at spotting openings that others ignore or identifying opportunities others can't see and then rapidly building prototypes to get customer buy-in and feedback. They use a cyclical learning and discovery-driven approach: identifying problems to solve, testing products and services, analyzing customer response and feedback, and using that information to iterate the products or services or to redefine the problem.

It's important to understand the difference between a startup and a small, new business. Startups are about testing the unknowns and the possibilities of implementing a unique concept to disrupt traditional business or provide a unique product or service. Startups scale. They have massive ambitions. Their intention is to replace the incumbents in their industry. They reimagine categories and markets in ways that others can't.

However, in trying to stay in the moment, startups often relegate branding and strategic planning to the bottom of their priority list, which seriously hinders their potential for sustainable and scalable success. Many startups also lack the discipline of established organizations and chase every opportunity to the detriment of their value proposition and business model.

The Best of Both Worlds

If the definition of insanity is doing the same thing over and over again expecting different results, most companies are insane. More so, they're risking their own survival by not understanding how to change and adapt to a fluid market or how to establish a brand with staying power. In my decade working to help startups develop a Nike-sized presence, perception, and identity, I've studied the key differences between the mindsets and behaviors of startups and big brands.

The business style of startups and established brands contributes to their individual success but can also limit their potential. Established brands are adept at putting the consumer first and building strong strategic foundations but usually aren't built to operate under conditions of uncertainty. Startups are structured to react quickly and nimbly to accelerate growth but are inherently unstable. That's why the tension between those two stages of a company's lifespan offers such fertile grounds for study. The following table gives examples of traits I've observed in both startups and brands. There's no judgment involved here. Each of these traits has their strengths and weaknesses.

Key Traits of Established Brands and Startups	
BRAND	STARTUP
Testing	Experimentation
Measurement	Learning
Building	Hacking
Budgets	Constraints
Establishment	Disruption
Revenue	Value
Outcomes	Vectors
Process	Framework
Structure	Flow
Stable	Adaptable

Balance

We can't talk about this tension without talking about *balance*. It is quite the buzzword right now. And while I'm not particularly in love with using it to describe what I mean by "balance of stability and agility," you're going to hear me use it quite often. So I think for a lot of us balance implies some perfect, immutable state where everything exists in a tension-free, harmonious environment. But it's not harmonious, and it's definitely not tension free. The kind of balance we're talking about is not measured with a scale; it's measured by what you define as success and what that success requires in the moment.

For example, in my years in the startup and innovation ecosystems, I had a lot of startup leadership teams that were focused on work–life issues without thinking about how the entire orga-nization can achieve sustainable performance. As a triathlete and serial entrepreneur, I firmly believe that everyone needs tension and challenge to grow. Building muscle in weight training requires you to constantly create tension in your muscles with the weights, followed by proper rest and recovery. A holistic approach is nec-essary to achieve results. The same thing applies to your team—if everyone has a dynamic and full life outside of their work, it's actu-ally a helpful and critical setup for both our ventures' success and people's happiness. The problem is that when you try to create pol-icies that target specific issues without thinking about the rest of the organization, you throw off the entire balance you're trying to create. It's important to understand that it's not a 50/50 issue or a targeted policy; it's understanding what your team needs to exist in the world inside and outside of work.

When I tell you that you should think like a brand and act like a startup, I'm asking you to look at the context of the dynamic envi-ronment you're working in and recognize what needs to be stable in order for you to be agile. We all see the pockets of stability that need to exist in even the most chaotic startup environments—bills need to be paid, your employees need to feel safe and secure, and you need to have clear communication channels with your stake-holders. Having a stable base of operations is what allows you to respond to opportunities and crises with agility.

On the other side of the equation, those of you who operate in what I think of as a "super stable" corporate environment don't have the inputs that stimulate growth, since they only work with one side and don't balance out with an opposing one. These environments need more tension to challenge their norm in a more agile environ-ment that can unlock the constraints the established policies and procedures create. Your experimentation needs to recognize those constraints and figure out how to create new opportunities within some of those boundaries. You may also need to test those boundaries and see what happens. Push where you need change and know when you need to accept the status quo.

The Customer Is Key

To be successful, companies need to internalize both the stability of established brands and the operational agility of startups. To do that, they must build around the customer's needs. Brands and startups alike must build their strategic foundations focused on their specific customer to help them thrive in a world of constant choice. Customers are the most valuable assets of a company.

A brand creates customer expectations, a perception of value, and a sense of identity. If there are several products on the market with similar characteristics, brand perception is what influences the customer's choice. How well your brand serves your customers directly influences your ability to compete and ultimately win.

Finding and maintaining relevance with the customer and market as the business and technology landscape shifts means creating a culture of innovation and learning, because what customers love today they might forget next week. And where there is a market opportunity, there may or may not be a way to own and dominate it. Being open to exploring the possibilities without being wed to a particular outcome is essential.

Mastering the processes that deliver value, establish relationships, and grow loyalty is what eventually builds the foundation for a successful and stable business. Keep in mind that this needs to be embedded in every modern company's DNA; this is not a one-and-done approach.

Laying the Foundation

Companies must focus on three foundational areas: The first area is framing your company's priorities and perspective for combined growth and sustainability as a core part of the organization's DNA. The second area is strategy, which is essential to gaining and maintaining a winning edge. The last are the tactical essentials of operations and infrastructure that will deliver the biggest impact for your customers and your company. This foundation is built on the whats and the whys so that you and your team have the right mindset and behaviors to adapt to any circumstances and opportunities.

Of course, it also comes down to the alignment among these three areas, namely, how the focus on each shifts as you grow. It is the tension between stability and agility that makes this model work. To succeed in the modern market, companies need to put customers at the center, internalize the stability of established brands, and operate with the agility of validated startups. Combining the best of the two approaches helps organizations identify the short-, mid-, and long-term decisions, investments, and trade-offs to their initiatives to achieve and sustain ambitious growth goals.

Thinking like a brand and acting like a startup means borrowing the best of what brands and startups each do well and cutting out the parts that do not add enough value in a customer-driven economy. This hybrid mindset helps startup leaders gain a complete view of their growth and planning. The ultimate outcome is to build the growth engine for a new venture, facilitated by a high-performance team and proper insights to help them to focus on what matters most. Mastering these foundational concepts and capabilities creates the conditions for startups to thrive in the current environment and prepare themselves to deal with every crisis that the organization will undoubtedly face.

It seems like a lot, I know. But don't despair. Once you master the basics, you'll see that it's not that difficult. I'll walk you through the tools to think differently about the why and the how of your business. Once you commit to questioning your assumptions and embracing new ways of work, you'll be prepared for whatever the world throws at you.

Personas

It can be tricky to provide real-world examples of how I believe companies fail without violating an NDA, offending customers, offending friends, or losing said customers and friends. So I've created two company personas based on a real startup, corporate venture and individual experiences. They are situations that I (or my colleagues) have experienced to give you true-to-life examples, a practical application of the topics we'll cover.

Kevin at Big Brand

Big Brand Inc. is a vast, global, multinational brand that dominates its market. They are practically a household name and, in the past, have been industry leaders. The brand has come to embody quality and integrity.

They are the best at commoditizing and marketing products and services via incremental improvements and testing. However, their efforts at innovation have produced less-than-stellar results. Whether through acquisition or

continued

internal labs, they haven't had any breakthrough innovations in decades. They face new and increasing competition from established competitors and scrappy startups rapidly innovating in their market.

They've recently promoted Kevin, a star salesman and recent business school grad, to lead their latest innovation lab. Kevin's brief is to create a team at Big Brand that will increase the company's velocity on the innovation curve. He must build a team that operates in a new way while still following all Big Brand rules and procedures, including hiring.

Kevin has been with the company for six years. Now in his midthirties, he feels like he's figured out how the org runs and what its goals and expectations are. He has recruited two members from sales and engineering staff for the team because he has good relationships with those functional department heads and understands how they operate and what they do.

He has been assigned other team members from different functional departments, for example, design, product, UX, etc.

The reporting structure is Kevin's biggest headache on this project. The project is being spearheaded by his boss, Megan, managing director of sales. He also has a dotted line to Samantha, who heads the product team, and Jim, who oversees finance.

Jamal and Sarah at Struggling Startup

Struggling Startup (SS) LLC has developed a product with a potential global market. It has generous funding from the public and private sectors and has landed a significant customer. But they can't seem to take the next big step closer to profitability and gaining a large customer base.

Jamal and Sarah founded SS. Sarah has advanced degrees in computer science while Jamal is an engineer with degrees in both computer science and business. The two met three years ago, when they worked in the same giant corporation. Their product is a potential game changer in the B2B space. Their competition is a large, well-established first mover in the market. They've built a crack team of developers, designers, and support staff, only some of whom are co-located. Their hiring policies reflect their espoused value—to make the world a better place.

The company's biggest customer is Jamal and Sarah's former employer. They have an excellent relationship with the department head who purchased their product, but she leaves at the end of the year, and the contract expires six months later. SS has yet to land that second big customer that would increase their credibility and market share.

SS is burning cash and daylight, shortening their runway, and risking startup death. Investors are getting impatient, customers are becoming concerned about the company's continued viability, competing products are in the pipeline, and Sarah and Jamal are worried about making payroll and paying vendors.

Part 1

Perspective

o build a foundation for innovation, we need to begin with the right perspective. When I'm advising a venture or an innovator, I break perspective down into three areas: leadership, performance, and the gap. I know, I know—this is not everyone's definition of perspective. But in my experience, your mental models of leadership and how you identify gaps inform every aspect of your organization's performance. This is what I call *perspective*. If you can keep your focus on these three elements, you will build the foundation for success. "But Lauren," you say, "what is the right perspective?" Well, it depends on what your goals as a founder or corporate innovator are.

Are you in it for quick acquisition or your next promotion? (You know who you are.) Or are you in it for the long haul, trying to build something that you nurture and that has a lasting impact on more than your personal bottom line? Answering these questions requires you to dig deep and examine what you believe about leadership, performance, and what I call *the gap*. These are each tremendously important. Without all three, startups lose their way: going for the low-hanging fruit instead of pursuing their core customer, drifting away from their values, missing opportunities, and leaving employees adrift as they look for leadership. Many founders find that one or all three of these areas hold them back as they gain traction and go from a big idea to building out a sustainable and scalable business.

Leadership

Whether your business is a days-old venture or a decades-old corporation, innovation and sustained growth cannot be achieved without competent leadership. A lack of leadership causes a myriad of problems, foremost of which is difficulty motivating and retaining employees, especially as the geographical barriers are being removed. How can a team keep their eyes on the prize when they're not sure what the prize is?

Performance

Performance is a combination of metrics and mindset. Focusing on the wrong performance metrics—or adopting a let's-scale-first-and-worry-about-profitability-later mindset—has doomed many a startup. Especially those who don't have $50M to pad their runway to enable the blitzscale outspend-your-competitor approach. Lacking a test-and-learn mentality will do the same.

The Gap

Identifying the gap between vision and execution is where your work begins. Which unmet need are you fulfilling? Which underserved audience are you serving? To put it another way, *Why did you start a business, again?*

Building strong leadership skills, focusing on performance, and being aware of blind spots give you the perspective you need to set yourself up for success.

Chapter 1

Leadership

I've founded businesses, been a managing director inside a major American corporation, and consulted with many different brands in many different industries. Let's remember that I started as a marketer—and I was damn good at my job. But when I struck out on my own as a consultant, I noticed something strange in many of my gigs.

Whether I was working with entrepreneurs, ventures, startups, or advisees, they would carefully lay out what they believed their marketing problems were. But when my team and I dug into what was happening, it seemed like marketing was the least of their problems. We discovered that often the problem wasn't coming from an individual department or function; the problem was most often a lack of alignment—that leadership was not effectively communicating what each department's goals were and how those contributed to the overall growth objectives and impact.

I'd see a lot of confusion around what the strategic objectives of the organization were, both between teams and even within teams.

For example, some teams were externally focused on the customers and the competitive landscape while others were internally focused on team or company processes. But neither team had a firm grasp on how their work achieved the overall strategic objectives.

If we were able to convince the leadership of the need, I would prescribe a program of internal marketing and clarifying communication types and channels, along with a discussion of what "good" or "effective" communication looked like in that organization.

But I didn't believe that was enough. What I was really seeing was a failure of leadership at a fundamental level. Most of the leadership focused on communicating what they thought the team should be doing at any given moment, where they succeeded, and where they fell short. But the harder work was making sure that the whole organization was providing the clarity that keeps teams aligned. We need community, culture, and well-being to keep people aligned and engaged to not only retain talent but help keep both the talent and the organization's growth sustainable.

When you're in the weeds of trying to build a business or run a successful team, it's easy to focus on immediate opportunities, fires to put out, or the tasks the team should execute rather than attaining specific goals. But it is your job to stay focused on the overall strategic objectives and to tie it both to the larger impact and the short-term execution to get there.

Staying focused on strategy is hard—believe me, I know. It's much easier to focus on whether or not each team member has hit all their performance goals. But that's not really your job. Your job is to create clarity and work with your leadership team, regardless of team size or structure, to provide the processes that focus all that work on the stated objectives, so you can be free to search for the next opportunity your organization should go after.

Staying focused on objectives is one of the hardest things I've had to do in my career. As innovators, it can be easy to get excited about an emergent opportunity that distracts the team or to focus too closely on the details. This narrow focus can feel gratifying, like you're accomplishing something—but that's the trap. You've (presumably) hired or recruited a team of talented professionals whose judgment and skills you trust (if you haven't, well, that's on you). You should focus on providing the right environment for them to exercise that judgment effectively. And that means having clear communication around the strategic goals of the organization, as well as creating solutions and a growth-oriented culture of inclusivity and psychological safety. This is the only form of leadership that's scalable. And if you do it properly, the clarity and forward trajectory can energize your venture's culture.

"Lauren," I hear you saying, "I have a shelf full of books written by great leaders—what more is there to say?"

I'm glad you asked. I've read most of those books, and while I often agree in principle with what they say, I often see their ideas fail in the real world.

I'm not saying there's anything wrong with those books. The people who wrote them are usually fairly successful. But those people aren't you. You're the one who has to create a successful strategy and culture for your team. You're the one who has to decide what that success looks like and how to get there. What I'm saying is that you can't just copy one of the greats. You can learn from them, but ultimately you have to find your own path and your own way of managing the expectations of your team, your stakeholders, and your customers.

I'm not going to tell you how to become the "best" leader. I will discuss what I've observed at the different companies I've worked for and with over the years—some good, some bad. Or more to the point, some effective, some less so. I hope these examples will help you think about what you're trying to accomplish and how *you* want to lead your team there.

I've seen many leadership styles: collaborative, coaching, democratic, bureaucratic, autocratic, sympathetic, empathetic, and more. What the successful ones have in common is that their leadership is a consistent reflection of the individual leader and their beliefs. They may read the leadership guides of their favorite tech gurus and even try some of the tips and techniques they recommend, but the way they lead their team reflects their core personality and values. In other words, their leadership style is rooted in authenticity. I know, I know—buzzword alert!

One of the most inspiring leaders I've met recently is Mariana Costa Checa, founder of a social enterprise. Her company, Laboratoria, is dedicated to empowering women from low-income backgrounds and providing them with the resources they need to train for and find a career in the tech world.

Latin America is one of the fastest-growing global tech hubs. In 2021, startups raised a total of $19.5 billion in funding. Even though Latin America has a reputation for being a difficult ecosystem to launch startups in because of turbulent political and economic contexts,[1] local entrepreneurs are not afraid to take on the challenge and solve complex problems, and Mariana is a clear example of a social enterprise transforming the tech sector in Peru and Latin America. She found the newness and rapid growth made the tech sector a better target for disruption than more traditional, male-dominated professions like finance or business.

Mariana is an example of the future of leadership: leaders who are mission-driven but who build spaces where the goals and visions are shared by everyone. As Mariana said during one of our conversations, "When you are the CEO of the organization, you also need to actively lead and be the person that sets the vision, the one who inspires and sets the standard. But you need to balance this with a space for leaders to arise, grow, and inspire others."[2]

Yes, she sets that vision, but the company's values and culture are created by the entire team: "There is a lot of codesign, and yes, I do believe it is a balance. If we codesigned everything, it would never end . . . But, often, it is worth the extra effort to involve the team, because, that way, they can own it."[3]

Born in Lima, Peru, Mariana spent quite a lot of time abroad, pursuing her bachelor's degree at the London School of Economics and later a master's at Columbia University. During her time in New York, she was able to closely observe the tech industry—particularly the web development business. Tech is one of the few sectors that values skills over educational credentials and certifications. But in Peru, the entire tech industry is almost completely male dominated. Even women with impeccable credentials are underrepresented, never mind those from the lower end of the socioeconomic spectrum.

When she returned home, she cofounded a very successful EdTech firm. But she never forgot the urgent need to increase the representation of women in the tech sector in Peru. Combining her insights from her time abroad with her experience as the cofounder of a successful software innovation firm, she saw an opportunity to create a successful business and generate a positive social impact on women who lacked means and access. In 2014, she founded Laboratoria as an EdTech company that provides a platform and training to women through a six-month, fully remote boot camp to build technical and life skills. The pilot program had six women enrolled.

Today, Laboratoria has more than 2,800 graduates, 1,000 hiring companies, 30,000 boot camp applicants, and has expanded to five more countries in Latin America (Brazil, Chile, Mexico, Ecuador, and Colombia). It also receives funding from prominent companies such as Google, Telefónica, BlackRock, and the list goes on.

Since the launch of Laboratoria, Mariana has gained global recognition for her work: She was named one of *MIT Technology Review*'s Innovators Under 35 in 2015, highlighted in the BBC's series *100 Women*, received a Business Leader of Change award, and was even selected by Mattel to have a Barbie designed after her for International Women's Day in 2019.[4] As if that wasn't enough, Mark Zuckerberg, at the Global Entrepreneurship Summit in 2016, openly expressed how "Women who go to Mariana's program managed to access the opportunities offered by the internet. That's the future I want to build," expressing how Laboratoria is succeeding in their goal and vision.[5] Former president Barack Obama also praised the high percentage of her graduates who managed to secure a position for themselves afterward.[6] With over 2,800 past and current students and an increasing employability rate reaching 85 percent, Mariana has pushed Laboratoria to become a huge contributor in striving toward equal opportunity in a growing number of countries.[7]

Mariana embodies the key characteristics of many of the best leaders I've worked with. For me, the most important leadership skills are questions of character. They crucially include authenticity, transparency, and culture.

Authenticity

Your team always knows what to expect if you lead as your authentic self. Their reactions are genuine. (Is there anything worse than being hugged by someone who's not a natural hugger?) Authentic leaders don't treat the team differently just because there's a big-shot investor in the room or because a high-level executive at a vital client company walks in. The team always knows who's showing up for work in the morning and what they expect.

Maintaining authenticity in leadership requires you to identify your values, understand how they impact those around you and your community, communicate them clearly and consistently, and live them daily. When properly nurtured, authenticity drives trust and success. And if you don't do it deliberately, your team will decide for themselves what your values are and act accordingly (and inconsistently). More than anything else, authenticity sets the tone for collaboration and culture. When your team knows what to expect from you, they will feel safer sharing their ideas and perspectives, which means you get the full benefit of their knowledge and experience. Isn't that why you hired them in the first place?

The word *authentic* can be a challenge. It invites the best that is possible, as well as being that dreaded buzzword. True authenticity is demonstrated,

> *More than anything else, authenticity sets the tone for collaboration and culture.*

not proclaimed. Frankly, I get a little nervous when someone asks me how to be more authentic. I can tell you how I practice authenticity, but that won't necessarily work for you. The reputations of authentic leaders are evidenced by what stories told about them demonstrate, how they connect and handle mistakes, their openness to feedback and disagreement in creating solutions, and their capacity to inspire followers.

From the beginning, Mariana faced overwhelming odds. First, she was a female entrepreneur in Peru's male-dominated, patriarchal society. I'm not even getting into what that requires, but believe me, she's tough. Second, her approach challenged long-held beliefs that traditional nonprofits couldn't be profitable and innovative while delivering the same high standard of excellence as traditional companies. Her approach to leadership is authentic, transparent, and innovative, and because of this, she attracts and retains top talent to Laboratoria and has held onto her vision of social impact and innovation.

Transparency

There's a delicate balance between authenticity and transparency in leadership. Transparency doesn't mean that everyone should know everything, all the time. In the context of information flow, it means that data is available at the right time and in the right way so that work that contributes to the overall company objectives is easily achieved. Part of a leader's job is to provide access to relevant information and to know which context to use it in. This is where knowledge management comes into play. Talk to members of your team about how they access information within and without the company. What are the challenges? Where does information flow and where is it siloed? Knowing and leveraging existing communication behaviors and preferences can create flow and support transparency even at scale. It's one of the reasons so many startups choose to use Slack and integrate other Agile tools, from Trello to Google Docs, into it. It's why Google Drive now has workspaces and has adapted some intranet-like information architecture to provide structure while staying nimble.

I've seen a number of startup teams cobble together knowledge access systems that fall apart when the team scales. To be transparent, you need to think about information flow and access early, build a system that can scale, and make sure no information lives with just one person—even you!

But transparency is about more than just sharing information. Mariana, for example, believes that transparency goes hand in hand with authenticity. "You bring your whole self to work, not just part of who you are, and you stay open, honest, and true while working there. Problems are placed on the table and tackled rather than staying hidden away."[8] But this can be a double-edged sword. Because of our gender and the circles we operate in, Mariana and I have both experienced times when we were attempting to be fully transparent, and our colleagues mistook that transparency for incompetence or weakness. The intimacy and dynamics of the group you're addressing may determine the level of transparency you offer.

I'm a big believer in asking questions and admitting when I don't know something. But, as a woman, I've learned that if I say, "I don't know" or "I don't understand," it becomes an excuse for people to doubt my abilities. But asking for help and dropping assumptions in the high-stakes world of venture-building is critical for success. So, sometimes instead of asking a question directly, I start a conversation designed to elicit the information I need, without sowing the seeds of doubt. I think my particular leadership strengths are to keep the conversations productive and to communicate from a perspective of best intent even in hard conversations. It's all about creating and maintaining forward momentum. It took me a while to develop this superpower, but I do know it's a power that benefits every leader. One of the ways I try to be transparent in my own companies is with my monthly, company-wide ask me anything (AMA) sessions. In addition to the daily standups, it's a way for the team to fill in any gaps in what they need to know. Sometimes I provide the answers, but many times the rest of the team knows exactly where the answer lies.

Mariana also reiterated that transparency doesn't mean that everyone knows everything all the time. It means that, at the right times and in the right ways, you tell your people what they need to know, share insight and perspective, and include them in the decisions they have a right to participate in. For example, I don't always share the full projected profit and loss (PNL) with all the people who are working on a venture. But in my consulting practice, I surprisingly found that breaking down an initiative's budget against fees boosted team morale and performance. Knowing all the costs with overhead expenses helped them drive profitability. Your people need to know the budget for their project, but overloading them with the full financial picture (which requires a degree in accounting) can paralyze a team with anxiety. I want my team to focus on the work and the impact, not on how the company is spending or investing its money. (Would sharing the burn rate improve the performance of the startup team? I don't think so.)

Culture

Everybody loves to talk about culture. Founders want to know the best way to build one, and innovation leaders in big organizations want to know the best way to deal with what already exists.

It's very difficult to create a company culture. According to Workhuman, "Only one in four employees strongly agree they feel connected to their culture, and only one in three strongly agree that they belong at their organization."[9] In the early days of a startup, I suspect the numbers are significantly in your favor, but as you scale, a healthy culture drives belonging.

As a leader, you create the conditions that will encourage the kind of culture you want to sustain. But a company or team is made up of individuals, and it's how those individuals interact with each other and the environment that determines what the company culture looks like. Don't get me wrong, you can certainly hire a bunch of sociopaths with a win-at-any-cost mentality—but that doesn't ensure a winning culture. It's likely that they would turn on each other and eat up their energy with internal toxic politics rather than defeating competitors in the marketplace. They will also eat up all your time and attention instead of allowing you to focus on the individuals who will execute your vision. I've found it works better to focus on creating an environment that allows the kinds of thought and work that I'm looking for to flourish.

CB Insights, a startup and venture intelligence research firm, is a great example of building a culture around shared values.[10] Their approach is based on employee growth and learning, so their company culture supports all kinds of learning and development, from traditional, structured courses to learning by doing. They even sponsor hack days, where employees are challenged to create something (an app, a location-based service, etc.). This fosters a sense of personal and professional growth while also creating innovative products and ideation for the company.[11]

By creating these educational opportunities and stipends, CB Insights attracts the kind of talent that flourishes in this environment, which has led to a hardworking, productive team and rapidly growing company with an ethos similar to its early days at NYU labs.

Mariana created Laboratoria to provide women in a patriarchal Peru with an environment that would allow them to develop their innate leadership and creativity. She knew that she was lucky enough to enjoy the privilege of such an environment in her own life, and she wanted to share that with others. Rather than shying away from the privilege she has, she learned to acknowledge it to bring new women into the spotlight and give space for new leaders to arise in her company. Because Mariana has so deeply integrated these values and humility into Laboratoria, she also attracts high-quality talent with the potential and willingness to grow. Mariana told me when talking about her company culture, "We've tried to build an organization where people can be themselves and we can all be genuine and that makes it a pretty transparent organization, there are no things that are hidden, but instead, it's open and on the table so we can solve them."[12]

But culture doesn't always work the way you think it does. I'm always reminded of a team leader whom a colleague was brought in to coach. He was a difficult case. Although he was a brilliant technician, he was abusive to his staff, disdainful of their efforts, and generally not very nice. When he was interviewed, he stated that the reason the team was having trouble getting work done was because they were lazy. In the middle of the engagement, he was fired (there are only so many times you can tell senior leadership that their idea is stupid). The new manager was the polar opposite—not technical but empathetic and caring.

My colleague reinterviewed the team to see how this change in leadership was affecting the workflow. Surprisingly, the team members all mentioned how much they missed their former boss.

"But he wasn't very nice to you," she said.

"No, but he really focused on our professional development," they replied. "He was kind of an asshole, but he was an asshole who helped us. The new guy is really nice, but he doesn't know how to help us do the job. And he doesn't understand anything about our professional development."

That was a lightbulb moment for the consulting team. It was less about the leader's personality and more about the value he delivered to the team.

I'm not advocating for bad behavior here. I believe that you should treat everyone with respect. In fact, I demand it in my own organization. But it was an interesting lesson in how leadership is perceived by the team. Being empathetic or kind or democratic or even autocratic will only get you so far if your team doesn't perceive the value of your leadership.

Decision-Making

Have you ever wondered how many resources and how much time you waste in making a decision? One of the top three consulting firms, McKinsey & Company, gave us a better idea of how inefficient we are, sharing that "managers at a typical Fortune 500 company may waste more than 500,000 days a year on ineffective decision-making."[13] That might sound dramatic, but it demonstrates the consequences of making ill-informed decisions on a daily basis.

We are used to seeing only the C-level employees making decisions in the organization, when, in fact, decisions should be made at the lowest level possible. My earlier days working with consumer brands reinforced this. Frontline employees who interact with customers the most often have the best understanding of both the challenges and the opportunities. Making decisions more inclusive and collaborative will allow for better outcomes. Bringing back the concept of culture and making sure an organization fosters effective and efficient decisions is key.

Let's look at an example from my consulting and startup CMO times. I was hired to assist with a product launch. My team and I created a product roadmap and scheduled a meeting to discuss it. After the sixty-minute meeting, the client told us they loved the proposal, but we needed to schedule another meeting with another manager because they weren't authorized to approve the decision. This made me question how much time and money is wasted when there is a poor decision-making process. In addition, technology has allowed for new communication channels to be implemented at big organizations, which can end up causing more meetings, emails, and disengagement before a decision is made. There needs to be a clear strategy—and in some cases, a clear hierarchy—when making decisions.

The most important thing I've learned as an entrepreneur and corporate executive is that when you are the leader, everything is a decision. You don't have the luxury of not doing anything. When you're in charge, not making a decision is the worst decision you could make.

To reiterate, decision-making at startups is usually focused on staying agile and seizing any aligned opportunity that comes along. They aim to avoid the waste of bureaucracy in favor of fast, distributed decision-making. And that works well for a while, but it usually doesn't scale, so when it comes to actually monetizing the opportunity, they fall short. Big brands have the infrastructure to train their employees to make well-informed decisions that align with the company's goal and metrics, but they often can't seize the next opportunity until they run it up the chain of command.

Each of these approaches has its own merits. But it is the balance I need you to understand: the power of a brand with the agility of a startup.

And Finally . . .

So, how do leaders think like a brand and act like a startup? What I've learned from my own experience in countless startups and the example of innovators like Mariana Costa Checa is that finding the balance between stability and agility is the real work of leadership.

In my practice, I strive to give my team a stable infrastructure that allows them to identify problems, build solutions, and influence or own decision-making. When I think of stability, I think grounded. Stable organizations have a track record of success within a structured environment. They have rules, regulations, and repeatable processes that meet business goals. And if you're part of a team within a big organization, you should take advantage of that stability to accomplish your goals.

Many startup founders view stability as synonymous with rigidity; their companies need to be able to turn on a dime, so they embrace a level of chaos. But no matter how quickly you need to be able to respond to the market, your team needs to know that their paychecks will be delivered on time, that the lights will stay on, and maybe that there'll always be coffee. That stability allows the team to concentrate on productive work: creating the products and services, removing the hurdles that impede this progress, and driving valuable outcomes that will take your company to the next level.

In larger organizations, that stability also comes with dreaded bureaucracy. Navigating that bureaucracy, using it to your advantage, and finding the "cracks that let the light in," as Leonard Cohen would put it, is the biggest part of your job.

Kevin at Big Brand

Kevin looks around the table at his new team and then down at his notes. He welcomes the team and gives an overview of the stakeholders' expectations, then outlines the objective and timeframes. After his twenty-minute intro, he looks around the table. "Any questions?"

"I have to say, this all seems very vague," says Tiff, the senior designer. "Shouldn't we define *innovation* before we decide how long it will take to produce it?"

"Also," Aria chimes in, "I don't understand how this is going to impact my performance—and my bonus—in the design department."

"Good point," Tiff says. "How are we going to report this team activity to our managers?"

Kevin is unprepared for these questions, and after noting them all down, he schedules the next meeting to provide answers. Then he staggers back to his office and schedules a meeting with Meg, his managing director.

"They came at me with all these compensation questions," Kevin whines. "They weren't interested in the project at all."

Meg fixes him with her trademark icy stare. "You should have all that figured out already. I think we both know how it affects their bonuses, but do they?"

"I was focused on project goals," Kevin says. "I thought we'd figure all that out as we go."

Meg says, "I don't know how you expect them to focus on the initiative when they don't know how this project adds value for them personally, much less for the company. You have to create an environment that allows them to find the opportunities we're looking for. If they don't feel stable and secure, they can't do their best work."

"I'll schedule some time with the different department heads to work out how the Innovation Lab will be accounted for, and I'll bring a first proposal. I should have done that first."

"Yes," Meg says. "Whether you realize it or not, the functional managers are also part of your team; important stakeholders you need to bring along on the journey. They're the ones who will have to figure out how to operationalize any products or services you come up with. You'll still need buy-in even though this is an 'innovation' investment."

Kevin leaves Meg's office feeling dejected; he doesn't have a clear idea of how to get started. He thinks back to his last management seminar and realizes he can have the team find answers to their questions collaboratively.

At the next team meeting, Kevin gets the ball rolling: "I know there were a lot of questions about how this work fits in with your functional departments. We're going to start collaborating on every aspect of the team. So right now, let's focus on aligning this new team with the Innovation Lab in order to give more clarity and set a good foundation from the get-go. A trajectory-building exercise around team functions and outcomes would be the best way to get us started."

He brings up a slide. It reads, "What does the team need to do to effectively create, build, or redesign a product or service?"

For the next twenty minutes, the team fills the walls with ideas, concerns, and comments on a plethora of sticky notes.

continued

Then they group them by similarity. After another twenty minutes, Kevin asks the team to sit.

"It looks like we have several action areas that need to be addressed," Kevin says.

Tiff calls out, "Maybe Aria and I could recreate this on a Miro board and put in a trajectory and timelines for things like the operations questions."

Kevin is delighted. "That would be great. Can you get it done this week?"

"Give us a few days, and we'll share our board. Everyone can include their reactions right there."

The session has given enough information to begin the process of collaboratively figuring out the team's place in overall operations. Kevin's ready to take the next step: meeting with all the functional managers to figure out a system.

Jamal and Sarah at Struggling Startup

Sarah and Jamal are sitting in her office with Nik, the product owner, who just criticized their team's progress in an all-hands meeting. It was Sarah and Jamal's first revelation that things weren't working out flawlessly.

"You guys okay? It got a little intense back there."

"Are we really that bad?" Jamal asks, half joking.

"I think you guys shouldn't take all this personally. It's more about the company's lack of progress. Everybody's frustrated, but no one's addressing the elephant in the room—and that's your job."

"What do you mean?" Sarah asks.

"Look, you two have very different approaches to leading the team, and frankly, it confuses us. Jamal, you set clear expectations, and you lay out beautiful timelines and plans. Sarah, you've got this awesome vision for how we're going to change the world. But either you two need to start connecting the dots for us, or let's work together to connect them. We need to tie together our strategic objectives, our ways of measuring success, and where to look for our next opportunities. We need to connect these dots to know what comes next!"

Jamal interjects, "We need to be flexible!"

"Right," Sarah adds. "We have a lot of competing interests here."

Nik says, "Being a leader is about balancing all those interests. Right now, you've got the team furiously trying to finish the new product while continuously adding new features to the older product. Which is the priority? Which of those activities gets us closer to our strategic objectives? More to the point, what *are* our strategic objectives? A vision alone is not a strategy. You need to tell the team how you plan to accomplish that vision."

"I feel like you're saying we don't know what we're doing," Jamal says.

"Not at all. You both have skills and are inspirational in different ways. But your distinct approaches really confuse us on what we should be doing now. We really need to know whether we're maintaining existing products or building new ones. If it's both, then how do we allocate resources?

continued

Are we okay with doing both more slowly? Or are we okay with the trade-off of prioritizing one?"

"So, what do you think we should do?" Jamal asks.

"Do you remember that workshop we went to a couple of months ago? The speaker talked about how leaders need to balance the stability of big companies with the agility of startups. I think we need to start thinking like that. We have the agility part down, but we're missing the stability that clarity and objectives provide."

"How do we get there?" Sarah asks.

"The exercise we did at that workshop might be a good place to start," Nik answers. "It's called the Golden Circle.[14] It explores the why behind a company's 'just cause.'[15] The goal is to elicit the various perspectives on the company's values to see if they align. I think you two should run through it to settle on the most effective leadership style you can manage together. Your approaches are so different that it creates uncertainty. Are we Jamal's troops or Sarah's family? They don't gel."

"I found a description of the exercise!" Sarah exclaims. "You start with the 'why,' then the 'how,' then the 'what,' and each informs the rest as you progress. If Jamal and I do it together and then extend it to the full team, we can see if we're on the same page. If not, we can see what we have to work on to get there."

"Exactly," Nik replies. "That will get us started, but it's only the beginning. You two have a lot of hard work to do on your decision-making framework and how to share it with us as a team. You also need to come up with a set of uniform performance metrics, so we all have a clear definition of success. But that's a different conversation."

Chapter 2

Performance

Performance is the life force of any and every venture. When I was thinking about how to talk about thinking like a brand and acting like a startup in terms of performance, I struggled to find the right metaphor. Ripening fruit? No. Construction projects? Not quite right. Surgery? Ugh, absolutely not! But then I thought, *Boats!* "Really, Lauren? Boats?" I hear you. But bear with me.

Big brands are like battleships: They're massive, gleaming, and packed with crew and amenities. They have enough power and fuel to travel between continents. These things are built to withstand a lot of destructive forces—even taking a direct hit. A vessel that big takes a lot of power and carefully crafted processes in order to move. No job is too insignificant, and no area of the ship is left to its own devices. Everything on board serves a purpose. There are standard operating procedures for everything, from how to order lettuce to how to maintain and operate the propulsion engines. And everyone from the lowest-ranked sailor to the captain knows and understands how they fit into the successful performance of the operation. Lessons are learned from prior operations to ensure the same mistakes don't occur on deployment. All personnel know that even the smallest detail can result in a potentially catastrophic situation and make the ship unable to execute its mission flawlessly.

But battleships aren't very nimble, and they don't do well in shallow water. There's really no turning on a dime with something that cumbersome. It's also challenging to institute changes on the fly. Those same processes and procedures that ensure the ship is running smoothly when everything aligns can create unexpected challenges when things go to hell.

In one such instance, the USS *John S. McCain* collided with the *Alnic MC* in August of 2017. The *McCain* was preparing to move through the Singapore Strait, and standard rudder swing checks were being performed per usual. (The rudder tells the ship what direction to go in; I know you know that.) Shortly after midnight, one of the radars malfunctioned. This is not a good thing. Controls were handed off five times in the span of two minutes, confusing everyone between engineering and the helm. The inevitable collision occurred fourteen seconds later, resulting in ten deaths.[1]

The ability to pivot in the middle of a mission is a challenging one. Decisions must be communicated both up and down the chain of command simultaneously. And while decision delegation is encouraged, when the proverbial shit hits the fan, the captain is ultimately responsible. The key to assuring mission success on these large vessels is training, knowing, and following standard operating procedures, and the ability to execute clear verbal and written orders to the letter. Any organization that has been around a while, like the US Navy or any giant corporation, has a history. The company has learned what does or doesn't work based on their objectives. There's a CEO at the helm providing a vision and mission, and there are critical processes that must be practiced and honed to near perfection in order to perform successfully. The personnel are trained, standard operating procedures are in place to assist, and of course, money must be made. This stability means that brands can continue to grow. At the same time, miscommunications, fatigue, and poor training may not lead to a metaphorical loss of life; instead, they may lead to poor execution of goals, decreased profit, and potential loss of business. It takes immense planning, coordination, and space for an established brand to change course. It can also withstand the power of many waves—icebergs, not so much.

Big brands are practiced at creating clear vision. This doesn't mean that the current state of each big brand is precisely what the founders envisioned; the flexibility and adaptability of a founder's mindset are super important. It does mean that the founders did an excellent job of maintaining a clear, focused vision throughout the growth process, reviewed and realigned it often, and effectively communicated it to their team, customers, and other stakeholders to achieve and maintain the venture's mandate. A proven, repeatable path to success requires careful consideration and studying of performance over time, as well as ongoing analysis of the critical factors in success and failure.

Most startups, on the other hand, are more like speedboats: They're small and lightweight. They are fast. They can operate in shallower water and navigate in tight spaces. That startup agility (thinking, understanding, analyzing, and moving quickly) combined with a willingness to experiment and fail are the startup qualities that brands should incorporate into their innovation strategies, venture portfolios, and operational ethos. And brands understand this, intellectually. But trying to institute those kinds of changes into legacy systems is like trying to turn a battleship.

Startups can crop up in any business environment at any time. Their focus is on providing a novel product or service, improving upon one that already exists, or creating a new category to compete with an existing market (take Airbnb going up against the incumbents of the hotel industry). They must grow and show, through repeatable processes and consistent delivery of their value, that they are capable of performing against their competitors. The startup manager must develop leadership and management skills from the beginning, as the startup must grow as fast as possible.[2] Finding, training, and retaining employees must be accomplished quickly. Employees must know and understand the highly volatile nature of the startup landscape. Typically, startups are founded by a small, tight-knit group who are all invested in the company succeeding. And, just as the Navy SEALs do, a startup's crew must be able to pivot, adapt, and overcome obstacles to successfully perform their goals.

"Leadership is not about being in charge. Leadership is about taking care of those in your charge."[3] In this case, that's the different teams on board the boat. Sound familiar? In the end, the accident wasn't a reflection of the capabilities of the ship or its failings but a judgment of the captain in the face of crisis.

While newer ventures may be more adept at the rough seas, startups and speedboats are also quickly swamped by bad weather and can capsize or be destroyed by one collision. Many startups dream of being as well-known and solid as a big brand, whether by hard work or luck or by the sweat and tears of their people. And they're right to want that; the combination of agility and stability is the only way to thrive in today's turbulent market.

KPIs and OKRs

Okay, enough about boats. When I talk about the balance of stability and agility in business, I usually focus first on what I consider the foundations, and from there I work outward toward the metrics that will measure my team's performance. And for the stable foundation, the first step is to establish your KPIs.

We're all business pros, so you know that key performance indicators (KPIs) are table stakes when we're talking about how to optimize performance. But how you choose and maintain those KPIs can be trickier than you think.

KPIs are quantitative measurements that tell us if we are meeting some desired outcome. They are derived by looking at the numbers. But how do you decide which measurements to use? And when should they change? People ask me all the time, "What KPIs should I use?" And my answer is, "You have to figure it out based on your context, market, goals, and ambitions. There are certain accepted standards about KPIs, but the bottom line is always, What are you trying to accomplish with this organization?"

I'm a big fan of KPIs that focus on the bottom line, a.k.a. revenue and cash flow. You may have a different goal in mind, but I like to make money when I'm running a business. And with declining venture stats over the last five years, I'm not the only venture professional who wants to see more than promise or traction.

Let's review how you can start to determine what a good KPI looks like for you.[4]

Your KPIs

- Should provide objective evidence of progress toward achieving strategic objectives.

- Should measure what is intended to be measured to help inform better decision-making.

- Should track efficiency, effectiveness, quality, timeliness, governance, compliance, behaviors, economics, project performance, personnel performance, or resource utilization.

• Should be balanced between leading and lagging indicators.

Once you've settled on your KPIs, you need some way to translate those into specific goals for your team. Unless you're in a specific niche business, you can't really give individuals goals like "generate $50K in the next quarter." Instead, you find objectives that serve your KPIs and goals that your team can actually meet. The $50K in net new revenue is just one specific outcome that adds some validation to the overarching KPI.

My favorite tool for this translation is OKRs. Objectives and key results (OKRs) create an analytical basis for decision-making and help focus attention on what matters most. KPIs are critical to measuring progress toward an intended result and are usually accompanied by a colorful dashboard and are continuously updated. OKRs are typically managed every quarter and are focused on more short-term goals. But they do bubble up and are used in a balanced scorecard, which connects the dots between the big picture (mission, vision, core values) and the more operational KPIs.

But remember: It is crucial to align your company with the right sub-objectives. Just deciding on a few OKRs and listing them out isn't enough; they need to be properly understood, integrated, and referred back to. Music streaming company Spotify actually realized how important alignment with OKRs is and even went so far as to curate their own performance framework. Spotify realized the power of aligning their OKRs to their North Star (their main goal as a company) rather than isolating their objectives. In their case, they found that their company would suit a new framework, combining the North Star and OKRs into what they called Spotify

Rhythm.[5] But you don't need your own framework to see the same success as Spotify. What you can take away from their strategy is that outlining OKRs independently will fail to provide any value to you. They exist to align toward your North Star and are then referenced when your people work through some of the finer processes or projects. The OKRs aren't simply another thing on the to-do list to make your business seem more accomplished; they are a tool that can help you.

Leadership Qualities

Successful business professionals appear to have similar qualities. While they may be unique in attitude and execution, these traits carry across enterprises and are viewed as essential characteristics to have or build upon for success.[6]

The first definitive characteristic is a clear and prioritized vision and goal. This needs to be set in order to inform your decision-making and plans for the company. Staying focused on a daily basis is simple yet effective and can ensure that the finite amount of time and energy you have is spent well. Some people choose to stay focused through SMART goals, producing outputs that are specific, measurable, achievable, relevant, and time-bound. But there are many ways of staying informed and focused in decision-making. Even reflecting on what decisions you've made in the past can help you move forward, so it's trial and error for what works for you. The key takeaway from this is to reestablish your goal and refer back to it continuously.

Second, a lot of people neglect the importance of their own personal health and lifestyle, especially during critical phases or venture inflection points, under the assumption that this is a temporary state and that they will have time to focus on themselves later. I have personally found it to be a slippery slope and have been hired to fix startups whose founders

If you lead a disorganized and unhealthy lifestyle, your business will reflect this.

and leaders made similar concessions and sacrifices and eventually caused fundamental erosion in their businesses. What might seem like a momentary and minor sacrifice can, over time, erode the culture and well-being of the business. While business and personal life will always be separate for the corporate innovators, as a founder it is inevitable that one will bleed into the other, or you may even choose to integrate the two. If you lead a disorganized and unhealthy lifestyle, your business will reflect this. Your health will determine the energy you can spend on your business, and focusing on basic healthy habits like eating well, exercising, and even maintaining a good social life will inevitably improve your well-being and the business's health. Imagine having to make an important decision while your personal life is hectic and in shambles. Not likely to end well, is it?

The next characteristic is something we are hopefully all aware of already: putting in effort to grow and improve at all levels—personal, team, and organizational. You might have already implemented tools and methodologies like Lean, Six Sigma, or Agile, and this can be useful in measuring the current operations in the company, but just because you have this nailed down doesn't mean you stop there. Entrepreneurs and innovators need to continuously learn and grow; it's at the core of every industry leader and ingrained in how the world works. Thinking critically, multitasking, and looking for new methods and innovations can result in a better awareness of your market and give you a better vantage point.

The final point is understanding that having a work–life balance does not mean it's a 50/50 split at every moment. Work is an extension of your life but should in no way control it. Successful entrepreneurs do spend a lot of their time and efforts dedicated to innovation, but by no means should they sacrifice their day-to-day activities and social life in pursuit of it. The two sides can coexist; being a successful founder doesn't automatically disqualify your personal life. If you surround yourself with constructive and like-minded people, you'll quickly find that having a healthy personal life will indirectly fuel your work, creativity, and inspiration as well.

Once we understand the key factors that maximize performance as an entrepreneur or innovation specialist, how do we implement them in our businesses? It's metrics and measurements to save the day! In tech, we're known for tracking everything, from how many widgets we can make daily to how long someone stays on the website. And, of course, we need statistics! I heard it once said that statistics can either support or illuminate. It's true. Numbers are supposed to be black and white—a number is a number. However, creating performance metrics is a whole new ballgame!

A Case Study: Me

We've all asked ourselves—and I keep getting asked—how to measure performance. It's a good question that I wish I had a straightforward answer to. But the reality is that the answer is, of course, it depends.

So to try to tie this all up, I'll tell you how I have used KPIs to run my business and used my favorite measurement tool, OKRs, to measure the changes in the business.

I have almost always had what is now called a *distributed team*. No matter where I've been based, my team is usually all over the world. My assistant and one of the designers were in Latin America, the copywriter was in San Francisco, the marketing strategists were in NYC, the dev team was in Europe, and I was wherever my current consulting job or venture was based. You get the idea. As a result, we have always been very early adopters of a variety of different communication tools.

With that constant distance, how do I keep the entire team aligned on the vision I created for the company? I am obsessed with profitability. In any company I've run or advised, I've always been focused on how to increase revenue and create a profitable cash flow and, as a result, prompt value-creation. So my KPIs are things like the cash-to-liabilities ratio, cash flow, revenue, and net profit growth.

So what would my OKRs be? Let's take a simple one: revenue. The objective is to increase revenue, perhaps by a certain percentage. Telling the team that we should increase revenue is just making a demand (and if you hired great people, it should be obvious to them). The question is what measurable key result would help us increase revenue. For the consulting practice, it was often something simple like new customer acquisition or existing projects. Each of those has a different impact on the income, margin, and, therefore, profitability, but they are both important key results for the revenue and net profit KPIs.

I usually have two or more tiers of OKRs for my team: There are the high-level business impact ones tied to things like revenue, but there are also project-level OKRs that are tied to things like customer satisfaction, project completion, costs, etc. These are always tied back to at least one KPI (customer satisfaction impacts customer retention levels).

There you have it: a brief overview of how I use KPIs and OKRs to balance the stability that I need to grow my business with the agility my team needs to better respond to customers and get the job done effectively. Performance metrics are always a work in progress for me. While this isn't how I always operate, it is a window into how I try to think about what performance means at different levels of the organization.

And Finally...

By now it is clear that KPIs and OKRs are a crucial part of every founder and entrepreneur's journey. But let's remember that it is not just about copying the metrics of some successful enterprise. It's about finding the right metrics that float your boat. Are you (or do you want to be) a massive enterprise that can take a direct hit but can't maneuver out of the shallows? Or are you that sleek cigarette boat zipping across the water that's swamped by every wave? As you've seen, it's not an either/or proposition. Successful startups, teams, or innovation labs are the ones that know how to measure for stability and execute for agility.

Kevin at Big Brand

Kevin wonders if he's in trouble already. The innovation team is barely off the ground, and Jim has already called a meeting with the MD stakeholders. Jim is on the screen from London, but Megan and Samantha are in the room, along with a man who briefly introduced himself as Kris.

"I've been thinking about how we're going to measure the performance of Kevin's team," Jim begins. "Kris has worked with big companies, startups, and innovation labs

continued

and has a deep background in metrics and analytics, so I thought he could help. We need to determine how we measure the innovation team's performance. We have a lot of organization-wide KPIs, but I'm not sure how a new team will be able to hit these goals or translate them."

Kris looks around the table. "Jim has filled me in on expectations for the team and the enterprise KPIs. I'm interested in hearing what you guys think this project is about."

"It's about staying on the cutting edge," Samantha says.

"We need new markets and new revenue to fulfill our growth projections," Meg adds.

"I'm not sure," Jim begins. "Sometimes I feel like it's just something senior management feels you're supposed to have."

Kevin has never heard the MDs be this honest about why this innovation team was formed.

"Hearing Meg, Samantha, and Jim just now," Kevin says, "I'm not really sure anymore. My team is worried about how their work will impact their own performance metrics and reviews with their functional managers. I don't know how to satisfy everyone's needs." He slumps in his chair.

Kris says, "If no one knows the expected outcomes, how can you know what KPIs to use? And how can Kevin know what goals to set? What will success actually look like?" He shakes his head. "Before you start measuring, you need to start defining."

"But we have to address the enterprise-side KPIs," Samantha says.

"I'm not saying that you have to abandon the KPIs." Kris sighs. "As the senior management on this project, you have to set the expectations for the higher-ups for ROI and delivery. You also have to work with the C-suite and the functional managers to determine how you're going to measure success and give credit when the innovation is in production.

"Once it moves into production, all the revenue and profitability accrue to the business unit. For the innovation team, it becomes, *What kind of growth are we looking at, and what is our time horizon?* You have to determine with the functional managers how this work is reflected on the team's yearly review. You will never get someone's best if they're not getting credit for their efforts. You have to assess how the KPIs and other metrics serve your definition of success."

"Yeah, it would be interesting to take the time and define the time horizon we're trying to reach," Jim says. "Are we looking at incremental innovation or more of a moon shot innovation to get there?"

Kevin feels his stomach beginning to unknot. He feels like Kris really understands what he's been going through as he tries to balance the demand for innovation with measurements designed for existing production systems.

"Well, you've given us a lot to think about, Kris," Samantha says.

"But don't just think about it," Kris replies. "If you want Kevin and his team to have any chance of success, you have to change. You don't get the benefits of something new without the pain of losing something old."

"While we've been talking, I've set up a spreadsheet with all the current KPIs and OKRs, and I see what you mean," Jim says. "Some don't make sense for something novel."

continued

"I know you can do this," Kris says. "It just takes patience and thought. You're well on your way."

> **Jamal and Sarah at Struggling Startup**

Jamal and his team are carefully laying out their growth projections for the next two quarters for the board, but he has barely gotten through his intro slide when the venture capital representative, Claudia, interrupts him. "Our growth trajectory is all well and good, Jamal. But when are we going to see revenue projections? We believe in what you and Sarah are doing, but we don't have a blank check on this project."

At that point, Sarah's dad, Johan, raises his hand to speak. At first, Jamal had been against Sarah's dad being on the board—family and all that. But Johan has been in the tech industry for over thirty years. His understanding of the industry and his contacts have proved invaluable. Jamal reached out to him to find backend engineers and was delighted with the team that Johan had helped him pull together.

Johan clears his throat. "I've asked Desiree, my company's CFO, to review the financials you presented last quarter. Des has experience in the day-to-day operational metrics that newer companies need to keep an eye on. Des?"

"Okay, Johan. First, I've seen some serious missteps in the kind of KPIs you're concentrating on. A lot has changed in the landscape in the last couple years, even with investor patience on burn rate and profitability. You need to focus on revenue and cost metrics. Growth is an input, but it doesn't equal profitability, and that's what Johan and the rest of the board are expecting. Your customer acquisition costs are about 14 percent higher than the industry average for the startup stage you're currently in."

Claudia looks annoyed and briefly turns off her camera. Johan looks pained.

"I know you focus on your OKRs, and that's great for judging your team's performance against your day-to-day objectives. But you two need to focus on the KPIs that keep your business running. I don't see any realistic revenue projections in your finances."

"I've read a lot of startup books and blogs," Sarah interjects, "and they all said to focus on growth first, and then revenue will follow."

"We're not saying that growth shouldn't be an area of focus," Johan explains. "It's a leading indicator, but it's not the only thing you should be measuring your traction against. Scale without a path to profitability is useless. You need to find a sustainable way that doesn't require more investor capital to cover the gap."

Desiree says, "Maybe we need to be clearer in our choice of OKRs and then define whether we want to break them down into monthly, weekly, or daily goals."

"But won't that be really disruptive to the workflow and disorienting for the team?" Jamal asks. "They're already complaining about some of the OKRs. If we try to change them, the team might react badly, and it'll turn them against us."

"I think you'll find that, when you identify which KPIs you need to focus on as a team, your team will react positively.

continued

It will give them a sense of clarity and purpose that your current setup doesn't really deliver," Johan says.

Claudia has turned her camera back on. "Desiree, could you help them structure KPIs that tie to the bottom line?"

Johan interrupts. "I think the most effective use of everyone's time is for Sarah and Jamal to look at some resources Des and I will provide, work through some KPI and OKR restructuring, and then we'll give them feedback."

"That would be great," Desiree says. "I hope you realize that our critique is based on our collective experience in both the business and startup worlds."

"Actually," Sarah says, "it reflects a lot of things our team has been telling us they need to work more effectively."

Jamal adds, "I see a way forward. Sarah and I are grateful to all of you."

Chapter 3

The Gap

I promised my editor that I would not start this chapter with a joke about the global clothing brand. Instead, I'll start with a phrase I heard often in my years in London: "Mind the gap." This refers to paying attention to the physical space between the edge of the station platform and the train doors. Failure to do so can trip you up or, worst-case scenario, kill you. But the gap we'll discuss here has nothing to do with the London Underground; rather, it represents the disparity between the *vision* you have of what you and your company do and the actual *execution*. How does a founder or innovator bridge the space between these? It is often a question of perspective. How do you judge what you are doing and how that affects your outcomes or goals?

Of course, there isn't just a single gap, one thing you can tackle all at once. Gaps are everywhere. The question is: Which ones will prevent you from achieving your goals? You need to constantly be aware of the gaps between what you think is happening and what is actually going on. It is also a dynamic, ongoing process, not a single solvable issue. Identifying gaps is not a solitary activity; it requires multiple points of view on any given question. Some gaps are easier to see than others—if no one is buying your product, you may have found a customer experience gap. But others are tricky; it's human nature to focus on what you know (or think you know) about a situation. It takes work to uncover the gap between your experience of reality and the experiences of those around you.

Why It Matters

According to the firm Forrester, there is a direct correlation between customer satisfaction and loyalty.[1] A customer who feels valued will return. A customer who feels their needs have not been met will not. This should be somewhat obvious, but damage to brand image is not always immediately apparent—it builds over time. Losing a customer here or there isn't the end of the world, but allowing your reputation to erode could be.

According to a study conducted by SuperOffice in 2023, customers will pay up to 86 percent more for better customer experience (CX). Remember, too, that it's not just about customer service. Everything from product design and sales to post-sales support contributes to the customer experience. Why are we willing to pay a premium for an iPhone or a Mac computer? The seamless operating system and device ecosystem—that's all CX! And it makes all the difference. Companies that invest in CX have the potential to double their revenue and stand out from their competitors.[2]

It all starts with authenticity—just like in leadership! The human connection is the bridge. Your marketing can serve as an advocate for both business and customer. Ensure your marketing is in line with reality—that is to say, don't mislead your consumers. You can tap into their aspirational desires, but if you can't deliver on what you promise, you've just created a gap! On the social media marketing side of things, strive to strike a balance between brand advocacy and self-promotion. Customers will tune out when all they receive from you are poorly disguised advertisements. Advertising is not the problem; it's bad advertising that's sucking our precious energy. But if you have an interesting story to tell about your brand, your employees, or your company culture, they'll listen. We all love stories! We grew up with sci-fi and fantasy films and shows. Even with all the tech now, children are still enamored with stories. The film industry is estimated to be a $90 billion business due to the captivating drama and human appeal it offers to adults.[3] And despite facing increased competition, online streaming is still thriving, with an expected annual growth of 19.3 percent over the next few years.[4] Being able to deliver a story to our customers is a crucial component to engaging with them.

Deliver what you promise, and promise to deliver more as time goes by. Learn what your customers want, and offer as much personalization as you can. According to the firm Accenture Interactive, their Personalization Pulse Check (a survey of consumers) reports that 91 percent of customers are more likely to shop at locations that provide them with personalization options, such as relevant offers and recommendations.[5]

You can only achieve customer satisfaction if you eliminate the specific gaps between your vision and reality. There are two areas that are critical to understanding how those gaps arise and how you can identify them.

> *Deliver what you promise, and promise to deliver more as time goes by.*

Perception

Gaps often arise because of a core issue with perception. Whether you're the founder of a tiny startup or the leader of a large innovation lab inside a giant multinational, leaders are always accountable for maintaining as clear and accurate a perspective as possible. In marketing, perception is the first part of everything. Perception is a big part of the promise that each company makes to its customers. The difference between one's perception of their current state (what they believe is happening) and the reality of the actual situation can be enormous.

For example, I've had more startups than I can count tell me, "Our customers love us. We're totally customer-centric in our approach." But when my team and I dig in and come face-to-face with customers, we analyze not just sales but also social media and customer service calls, and it turns out that most of their customers don't even like them that much. When we sit down with the team, it turns out that the customer experience the leaders envisioned was just that: a vision. It hadn't made it into the execution of the product.

Biases

The underlying cause of many gaps is bias. Innovation leaders who work hard to uncover their assumptions and biases have clearer perspectives and higher rates of success. If you're a founder reading this book, you're likely dedicated to creating and scaling a successful venture.

Perception is inherently biased, which is why it's extremely important for innovation leaders to work hard to clear their own biases. It's hard for me to talk about bias without talking about the COVID-19 situation we all experienced worldwide, especially since part of this book was written during that time. Whether you're reading this book right after it's published or years later, you surely remember this time clearly. In the early days of the pandemic, people were counting down to a return to "normal." Further in, the discussion began of what the "new normal" would look like. At six months in, most people had accepted that there would be a "*new new normal*" on the other side of the global health and economic crisis we were living through. This is all a matter of perception.

If you've read a Malcolm Gladwell book, you're likely familiar with how bias drives much of our behavior on conscious and unconscious levels. Conscious biases manifest as preferences (maybe you only like purple Skittles, which makes you a maniac in my opinion, but that's my own bias). Unconscious biases, by definition, are much more difficult to identify than conscious ones. But identifying them is essential to success. For better or for worse, this is a hill I'm often willing to die on.

You might also be familiar with *kairos*, the ancient Greek word for "time," but in the qualitative, intangible sense rather than the more concrete *chronos*, which is sequential or chronological (etymology!) time. Kairos could also be interpreted as "the right moment."

In its essence, it is the correct, critical, or opportune time for something to happen. (Kairos also happens to mean "weather" or the plural form of "time," as in "the times.") All very appropriate for us to be examining in turbulent times. If you develop an expansive vision and the right perspective to spot the next insight, trend, or opportunity, and have the drive and ability to act, you can really innovate.

How does kairos connect with bias? An innovation leader needs to think about kairos and unconscious bias at the same time. If you really want to see every potential opportunity and every customer perspective, you need a lot of eyes looking out. If all of those eyes are the same—if they look and think and act the same—they're only going to be seeing a fraction of what's out there. Even if there are fifty of them, they will all be looking at and evaluating options in the same way. Your team should reflect your customer base; otherwise, who's really speaking for the customer?

We instinctively seek feedback and advice from our friends and peers, but most of our inner circle is probably a lot like us—like attracts like. Too often, we end up only finding voices that echo our own assumptions and biases, which compounds the problem by leading us to believe that pretty much everyone thinks that way and experiences life that way. Our family, friends, cofounders, and student networks—the people we trust and spend the most time with—often have a good deal of overlapping perspectives. Sure, there may be a few outliers in terms of identity and life experiences, but essentially it is a homogenous environment, one we see replicated and intensified in the business world.

In startup and innovation work, our biases and the resulting assumptions can lead to trying to build a skyscraper on a faulty foundation, or building the wrong product. I do a good amount of assumption mapping with founders and corporate innovators to ask, "What are the assumptions we're making?" followed by, "Is this assumption true?" and "Why?" to unearth the cracks in the company's foundation.

It's interesting how many successful tech entrepreneurs went to the same schools, were funded by the same VCs, hired the same engineers, dressed similarly, and even vacationed in the same spots. Or is it? For far too long, this was a self-selecting crowd, and as like attracts like, this homogenous crowd of like-minded geniuses perpetuated a cycle, intended or not. It's also likely how the idea of e-scooters became a major solution for the climate crisis. They had no perspective, which limited their ability to embrace kairos. They missed opportunities.

This is where a company's homogenous approach to prob-lem-solving and customer happiness shoots them in the proverbial foot. It's like trying to defend a castle from attack with a bunch of soldiers who only look in one direction. The enemy *will* sneak up on you. If you have all kinds of people looking in all directions, for all types of attacks, you are much less likely to be surprised. Companies have failed big time in having one perspective versus having all kinds of people looking in all directions. Big brands have failed to recognize their own biases, with single-minded perspectives. They therefore took on major projects and ran programs with a mindset unable to meet the real needs of their diverse customer base.

Types of Gaps

Whole books have been written about the gaps between perception and reality. And we just don't have time to explore the whole topic. But it's still essential to building a viable new venture, so here is a brief overview of the types of gaps that I have seen that damage the prospects of promising startups and stall the progress of corporate innovation teams. Even more convincing is that companies with above-average diversity perform 19 percent better financially than those with below-average diversity.[6] Although I'll only be men-tioning a couple of them, be aware that there are many ways to "mind the gap."

The Diversity Gap

I won't attempt to solve tech's diversity problems here. If I could, I would, and then I would immediately retire. But if you've been paying attention, you know that this problem is big.

I'd like to address one aspect of the diversity gap that is very personal. As a woman who has worked in the tech space for most of her career, I've often been told what I can't do. As a result, I have sometimes limited myself to what seems attainable. Instead of building a company that required raising outside capital or gunning to build a tech unicorn, I was funneled toward marketing roles that leveraged my brand and journalism skills. In 2005, I didn't have the mindset, role models, or mentorship to found a company, and the people who should have been enabling me discouraged me from doing so.

My female founder friends are still plagued with discrimination from VCs and board members. In 2020, startups founded by women only received around $5 billion in VC funding, while startups with both male and female cofounder teams received around $20 billion.[7] Although women have founded 38 percent of US companies, they only get 2 percent of the venture funding.[8] Shocking, no? Consider this the next time you are trying to craft "diversity initiatives." While you may think the gaps have been closed, they are still big enough to drive a truck through.

But diversity gaps exist inside your organization as well. One of the first decisions you make as a leader is who you hire. The tech industry has taken swings at addressing its own homogeneity but hasn't yet been really successful. Why hasn't it been successful? *Because it takes time and effort.* And hiring people is not what drew you to innovation in the first place. Recruiting and retaining staff can be tedious, uncomfortable, and messy. It also means knowing and owning your own biases. But it is a critical exercise because it involves tackling underlying belief systems. It's not just diversity for diversity's sake. It's addressing the biggest gap—and most common stumbling block—in innovation.

Diversity within bigger brands is something that startups can learn from (and I'm not saying that big corps always get this right).

Founders think they don't have time to find the right people. *They need engineers, so why not just hire their two friends who happen to be engineers rather than start a new hiring process? So what if they all think the same way—that's what you want, right? Just get them on board and build!* Don't let this be you. Don't sacrifice long-term success because you've bought into the idea that it's a problem you can fix later.

Invest in your long-term plan from the jump. You might be surprised at the value that different perspectives can bring at the earlier stages of discovery and development. This is the exercise that most often gets swept under the rug, and if you make it to big-brand status, you'll then spend hundreds of thousands of dollars trying to course correct and innovate. Instead, do it right from the start.

The Customer Expectation Gap

The customer gap is the difference between your customer's expectations and your customer's experience of the function performed for them. Your customers may not always understand what your service has accomplished for them, or they may misinterpret the quality of the service provided. And sometimes your organization is just not delivering on its brand promise. This creates a gap between the customer's expectations and their perception of value your team has delivered. It's a subtle distinction but an important one. It often comes down to not just *what* you delivered but *how* you delivered it.[9]

Many organizations are completely blind to this gap. It can be the result of other gaps in your organization (like customer service or process), or it may exist simply because the customer does not understand or perceive the true value of the service. In a worst-case scenario, customers no longer perceive any value in the offering, and your business loses a large percentage of your customers overnight.

Without awareness of this gap, companies risk losing a great deal to their competitors.

There are whole suites of tools dedicated to measuring how happy (and loyal) your customers are. I still use customer surveys, focus groups, and interviews to gauge how a startup's customers feel about them. But I also make it a point to interview individuals on every customer-facing team in the organization. It's important for you as a leader to remember that your team doesn't necessarily want to share bad news. I never ask about "happiness" in these interviews. Instead I ask, "What are your customers' biggest problems? What do customers complain about? How did they think the product would solve their problem?" The answers to these questions provide a foundation from which to analyze the gap between what the business is producing and what the customer is expecting.

In many organizations the next step is either to invest in a customer support department or invest *more* in the customer support department—especially as we enter the AI revolution and customers are beginning to seek even deeper connections to their brands. It's always amazed me how resistant companies often are to investing in the teams that are interacting with the customers at a make-or-break moment. This investment may be training or may be empowering the team to make decisions affecting customers in the moment. Customer retention is the golden ticket to marketers, and what better way to retain customers than to have problems solved in real time.

Assumption Mapping

We all know what happens when you assume, and now we have learned how our assumptions and biases affect our business. Assumption mapping is a helpful exercise to capture and challenge your potential biases and gaps and to create awareness around potential blind spots.[10] It is possible to check your organization's or team's assumptions! The first step is to make sure that those assumptions are challenged before they become unchallenged "facts" or the basis of your business. I use David Bland's assumption mapping exercise to kick this off.[11]

In assumption mapping, we ask ourselves questions about which of our assumptions have turned into "facts" that need to be reframed as hypotheses and tested as such. Both new and existing ventures should adopt a design-thinking perspective and examine each of these three key areas separately and together:

Desirability: Does the market want this? Fill in these blanks.

The problem our customers want to solve is

--.

What do your customers struggle with or what needs do they want fulfilled?

Our customers cannot solve this problem because

--.

What obstacles have prevented customers from solving this thus far?

The outcome that our customers want to achieve is

--.

What qualitative/quantitative changes will happen in the customer's life?

Viability: Is this financially worthy? Fill in these blanks.

Our acquisition strategy for obtaining new customers is

--.

What are your one or two main acquisition channels?

Our customers will use our products repeatedly because

--.

What will your customers come back to do and how often will they do that?

We will drive revenues by

--.

What is the primary way you will make money?

Feasibility: Can we build it? Fill in these blanks.

Our biggest engineering or technical challenges are

--.

What are the major architectural challenges that could get in the way of building your product or service?

Our biggest legal or regulatory risk would be

--.

Which laws or regulations could prevent you from operating the way you plan to?

Our team is uniquely positioned to win because

--.

What makes your team well-suited to beat the market?

Your answers to these questions are the assumptions you will now examine. Now draw a four-section chart with axes going from important <-> unimportant and known <-> unknown.

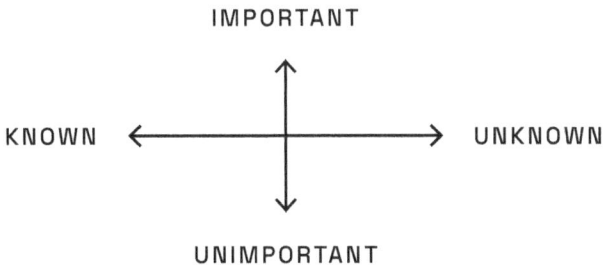

IMPORTANT

KNOWN ←——————————|——————————→ UNKNOWN

UNIMPORTANT

Now place your responses into the appropriate box. Did you know about this issue before you filled in the blank? Is it important to your goals?

Leaders often devote too much time and energy to challenging the responses that are both known and unimportant. Founders can waste a lot of time on these. The responses that fall into the known and important square are the ones you already have, and those in the unknown and unimportant square are the ones you don't need urgently—duh! They are unimportant. Where you really need to focus your energy is on the responses in the unknown and important square. Dedicate your time and resources to this section. These are your leap-of-faith assumptions, and since they are important, you need to dedicate time, effort, and energy to test these hypotheses and find out whether they're accurate.

Close the Gaps!

Close those gaps by listening to what your customers and your other stakeholders are telling you. The most famous statistic on this states that on average 80 percent of leaders believe that they are delivering a superior customer experience while only 8 percent of their customers believe the same.[12] This basically means that the average brand believes that almost three-quarters of their customers are getting a better experience than those customers think they are. That, my friends, is a big gap—the kind that can blindside any new venture and shatter your performance.

A continuous discovery process is necessary not only for constant improvement but to keep your lens sharp and keep you on top of new opportunities and innovations. It gives you clarity on the implications of recent or upcoming changes and the complexities of your vertical. For example, during the COVID-19 pandemic the sale of dry shampoo skyrocketed. Since most women were staying home, they weren't washing their hair as often and were using dry shampoo a hell of a lot more for Zoom calls. Similarly, when salons closed, women purchased at-home hair color in such droves that it led to restocking issues at several retailers. While no one could have predicted COVID-19 before it began, a savvy leader with her finger on the pulse of her customers' wants, needs, and habits may have been able to predict an uptick in demand for those products and could have been prepared—or could even have taken advantage of the opportunity by incorporating it into brand or demand-generation marketing. That kind of leadership is the difference between a company that survives and one that grows with amplified value. Every gap is also an opportunity!

And Finally...

I get it, Lauren. I GET IT. There are gaps everywhere! It's all chaos! Everything I've outlined here is to show you that you can avoid these gaps by creating and keeping perspective and by having your finger on the pulse of the intangibles with people. As I said, every gap comes with an opportunity to listen to your customers, listen to your team, lead better, and course correct to achieve your goals.

Kevin at Big Brand

Kevin is sitting in his backyard staring into space. He's thinking about a series of meetings he's had over the last two days and wondering how he got here. He met with the team to create a roadmap of objectives and deliverables. They came up with several innovative product enhancements that they could probably deliver in a calendar year.

This process was a revelation for Kevin. He had some idea of how the process worked at Big Brand, but the number of dependencies that had to be navigated, the processes to acquire resources, and the necessary approval procedures were startling. This was his first exposure to "how the sausage gets made," and it was daunting.

But Tiff, the senior designer, asked the questions that are haunting him: "Do the customers want these innovations? Are we working on the right things? Are we creating for the customers we have or new customers?" Her questions opened the floodgates as the team questioned how they were defining innovation, who they were innovating for, and on

continued

and on. Kevin scheduled a follow-up meeting because his head was going to explode and because he needed time to evaluate their concerns and find some answers.

Next, he met with the managing directors involved in the project. They wanted to know how the work was going and what would be delivered in time for the town hall at the end of the quarter. He said he'd back them on that but that the team was focused on a slightly longer timeline.

The meeting took a bad turn when Kevin brought up his team's questions.

"Just get your team on track," Meg said.

"There's a lot riding on this," Jim added. "We've put ourselves on the line for this initiative, and we need you to deliver."

Meg, whom he's worked with for years, made her not-happy face and scheduled another meeting for the next week.

Meanwhile, Kevin's getting a steady stream of emails from the functional managers wanting to know how these "innovations" are going to impact the existing product lines. The senior sales manager is concerned that changes will screw up existing customer relationships.

Kevin thinks back to a workshop on assumption mapping that he learned about from a startup speaker at his graduate program. He has the idea to run some of those exercises as a way to get everyone realigned on what they are building and who they are building it for in order to move forward. Of course, this is going to be more work. He's going to have to find the research and protocols and get the team on board.

Kevin decides his team needs to map the assumptions that underlie their definition of and approach to innovation. In addition to his team, Kevin should invite some of the functional managers, as well as one or two customer representatives if he can—or at least the senior sales manager. This exercise should result in better alignment with customer needs, expectations, and information that can be shared with the MDs and functional managers to set appropriate expectations about what *innovation* entails internally.

The next morning, Kevin and his team run the exercise. He's even able to pull in a few of his biggest customers. The results are eye-opening. The whole team is energized by the information they've visualized and the guidance the customers provided about what innovation means to them. Kevin is armed with data that will allow him to address the functional managers' concerns and the MDs' expectations.

Jamal and Sarah at Struggling Startup

Over at Struggling Startup, Sarah and Jamal are sitting in Jamal's office in stunned silence. They just got off a call with their investors, and it did not go well.

The lead investor told them about a new competitor that they just read about in *Fast Company* that was launching a product very similar to the one that Struggling Startup is introducing next year (almost exactly the same, really). The investors were upset that Jamal and Sarah hadn't included a disruption in the competitive landscape of their product

continued

roadmap. They wanted to know what SS's response would be. Can they drop the product sooner, or do they need to pivot?

The development lead said they might need more time; the release dates should be moved out. How did they miss all this? What are they going to do? Will the first move give either player a strong advantage? If they pivot, can they salvage all the work that's been done? How will the team react? What if the investors pull out in the next round of funding?

"Okay," Sarah says. "We've got to pull ourselves together and figure this out. We've clearly made some faulty assumptions about the market and our competitors. We need to measure the gap between where we are and where we want to be. We should do some assumption mapping, it might give us a stronger competitive edge."

Jamal replies, "I'm also going to ask Nik [the product owner] to investigate that competitive product."

The next morning, Nik reports that the product launch that the investor was talking about isn't really a competitive product. "It has some similarities, but what we should worry about is if the big boys start incorporating our features into existing product suites."

Sarah and Jamal convene the team to start assumption mapping their competitive landscape. "Okay, how did we approach the competition when we started? Is that still true?" Jamal calls his contact at their biggest customer and pulls him into the meeting virtually. As they work through the assumptions they made when they first started, the customer raises several issues that undercut their beliefs about what they're building and how fast they need to get to market. "I need something that actually works right away, not something that is updated every day for six months. That's what drives my team crazy."

Sarah and Jamal are exhausted but also exhilarated at the end of the day. "Wow, that was intense, but these insights are clear. Some of it validates our beliefs, but the challenges were the most useful part."

"I know," Sarah replies. "Nik's insight about what we should be worried about hit home. We have a lot to think about, and we should schedule an investor call so we can share all this and our course correction plan ASAP."

Part 2

Strategy

The strategy for any brand or startup is to build the right company, value, and offering. The strategic areas of the operating model include three pillars that will help you develop a winning strategy and a competitive edge. It also sets up the framework for ongoing strategic thinking, so you implement a learning, discovery, and then validation mindset that ensures you maintain and grow that edge. A common pitfall in both startup and corporate innovation is setting out on a mission to validate your idea or assumptions from the beginning, which just limits your opportunities, bakes in your biases, and limits your ability to de-risk new ventures.

Audience

It's not just validation and traction from your customers that will ensure a new venture's success; it's all of your stakeholders! Who is your customer? Is your organization reaching the right people? An understanding of customers, prospects, communities, stakeholders, market relationships, and what moves them to action (and eventually love and loyalty) is key to validating the effectiveness of marketing expenditures or product–market fit.

Brand

Brand has the power to humanize any company into a lifelike persona that audiences can identify with. Does your story resonate with your audience? Is it creating the necessary demand for growth? This is how we package up the benefits that help to create either premium value or some type of demand with the customers and other stakeholders along for the ride. Translating business vision into a cohesive experience requires grounding the key elements of a company identity in actions that deliver value to all stakeholders, especially employees and customers.

Category

Standing out in your playing field and gaining customer preference are the result of careful consideration of the strengths, values, and execution that set your business apart from the rest. Is your value proposition appealing, easy to understand, and communicated well? Category is all about understanding the market you're playing in, defining the playing field, and truly understanding the competitive forces at play. All too often, the definition of competition is where people stumble; it's either too narrow or too wide. Or people completely ignore the real or potential competition that could eat their lunch. In today's world of choice, knowing and monitoring your whole category, not just your direct competition, is essential to both gaining and maintaining a competitive edge.

Chapter 4

Audience

O ne of my earliest lessons in marketing was about the difference between a brand's customer and its audience. My mentor at the time was a big fan of Clayton Christensen's *The Innovator's Dilemma*[1] and the theory of Jobs to Be Done (JTBD).[2] She wanted me to focus on building the online audience for our beauty and wellness startup. I was arguing that our efforts at customer acquisition and retention built a big enough audience.

Over the course of several hours, she introduced me to the JTBD theory and how she used it to approach the distinction between customer and audience. JTBD defines the customer as someone who has a need that your product or service can fulfill and is willing to pay for it. The paying-for-it part was important.

Our audience was everyone who was exposed to our brand and either didn't have the need at that moment or couldn't afford to pay for it. Our mission was to make sure that our brand was always top of mind when the need arose.

That distinction between customer and audience has served me well over the years. It allows me to craft messages that resonate with those who purchase and those who wish they could.

I learned a similar lesson personally when I was a competitive swimmer when I was younger. If I remember anything it's how chaotic swim meets are: You're surrounded by your teammates, coaches, competitors, competitors' coaches, spectators, and, most likely, your parents. Oh, and the parents of your competitors. There are so many people around that it can be difficult to concentrate on what you're there to do, which, in a nutshell, is swim faster than everyone else in that pool. As a swimmer, I was there in that pool to swim the fastest and win the race with my parents cheering me on. But it actually went far beyond my supporters, and even the people present at the swim meet.

What I've learned—and what I want to share with you now—is that my audience included everyone in the competitive swimming ecosystem. After my win, I was approached by scouts, and our meet was featured in the local news. Our team was sponsored by a local business that wanted to leverage our success. That was my very first lesson in how broad the concept of an audience can be.

Presenting your company as a customer-first business is a popular approach in the current business world and startup ecosystem alike. Most founders already understand that their users (be it individuals or businesses) are a crucial part of the company's success and that serving them well from the start can lead to strong growth. But many founders don't clearly understand what business operations actually look like when you put your customers first or that it is your entire audience—not just your customers—that you need to identify, address, and communicate effectively with to grow your company as a brand does.

Through practice, I've also realized that it is essential to create one compelling message that articulates your value proposition to your entire audience. Segmenting your stakeholders and potential customer base is equally as important in order to deeply understand each group and communicate this same message to each one.

As a leader this is essentially what you do all day; you tell everyone you encounter what your company is all about. Everything that you say, do, build, manage, develop,

> *Everything that you say, do, build, manage, develop, and sell—all of it is in service to* **what your company is about.**

and sell—all of it is in service to *what your company is about.* This is the essence of a brand, and successful communication of your brand to your audience will empower you to grow your company with greater efficiency, power, and success. If your entire audience truly understands what your company is about, you can better move all of those stakeholders to action, and action, my dear friends, is exactly what you need to create and sustain a high-growth new venture. Put simply, you need these people to be bought in and to perform the actions you need them to execute in order to win.

Identifying Your Audience

Take a moment now to think about who your audience is. Consider all of the groups and stakeholders who see and interact with your message, brand, and product. Don't worry, I'll wait.

Thinking about the audience that you just identified, it's a lot more than customers, right? Your list should include your employees, who are your first audience. It should include groups as diverse as your suppliers, vendors, distributors, investors, shareholders, and press contacts, among others. If your list doesn't include all of these

groups, go back and rethink it to make sure that it is as compre-
hensive as it needs to be. Some of you may choose to add a board,
advisors, or investors to the above stakeholders.

Each of these groups is part of your audience:

- Internal stakeholders: your team, employees, and managers
- Connected stakeholders: distributors, customers (here they
  are!), suppliers, and shareholders or investors. It can also
  include former employees once your venture is big and mature
  enough that your early hires or equity holders have moved on.
- External stakeholders: government regulatory groups
  connected to your industry, the press and media, local communities, and society as a whole

I've listed the groups who are part of the technical definition
of audience, but they fail to include two additional groups who
will play a crucial role in your company's success: collaborators
and influencers.

Collaborators may not be the people buying your product or
service, but they are a support system that can boost sales and brand
awareness. This group can also include affiliates or partnerships that
drive awareness, influence, and sales. For example, if you're selling
fitness products, the opinions of health and fitness bloggers are
important, even if they are not part of your target customer base.
It's important to consider them when making decisions, because
they may have longer-term relevance in helping grow the business.
In our example of the world of wellness, having a blogger with a
clear POV and audience as an advisor and ongoing collaborator is
worth its weight in gold.

The last group is influencers. *Wait*, you might be thinking, *you just mentioned bloggers! Are you repeating yourself?* Not quite. This definition of *influencers* probably deviates from your perception of the term in that they operate on a macro level that's much broader than the reach of your traditional social media influencer.

Kim Kardashian is a good example. (I know, I know.) Kim does not blog or influence in the way that collaborators do, but her lifestyle decisions are reported in the news cycle. That is influence! Kim used the audience she gained through TV and social media to build an empire. Leveraging her influence, she created a cosmetics, skincare, and shapewear brand. All these products reflect the enthusiasm that her audience shows in her interests. The audience she built has led her to billionaire status.[3]

Now, we're not all going to get a TV show chronicling the antics of our crazy families, but the Kardashians are a shining example of the power and value of audience-building. Even if you're not on TV, you can create content that engages everyone with an interest in your project. Attracting an audience is just the first step. Next, you need to demonstrate how your product or service fills a need that the customer may eventually have (*I don't need shapewear today, but in a year or two, who knows?*).

So what do you do when you've attracted an audience? This is where engagement and messaging are critical. Your audience isn't one monolithic entity; it's composed of those who respond to different aspects of your brand messaging. Some may come because you're environmentally friendly, others because they admire how you do your makeup. But it is critical to identify which content each segment of your audience responds to.

The flip side of the rapport you build with your audience is that they are always watching you. That's right, they see you—both the good and the bad—and their judgment can be swift and merciless if you fall on the latter side.

For example, there have been recent cases of startup CEOs who used social media to message about discrimination, equity, and fairness. But then came the stories about bad behavior, ranging from dodgy financial practices to abusive behavior and outright sexual assault. The audience for these individuals and the brands they represent expected atonement and sometimes dismissal. You've seen the headlines.

You also need to remember that your audience and your customers are not static, isolated groups. They interact with your messaging but also with all the other stories that circulate about you and your company. They are often members of communities where they connect with each other over a shared interest in your solution or the problem it solves. This holds true for corporate innovators as well. Your team may be negatively impacted by stories that circulate about the larger organization. You must be ready to reinforce your messages not just to your customers but to your wider audience as well.

Another reason that this broad definition of audience is so important is that there is more transparency than ever between these groups, meaning that each of them has visibility into your relationships with the other ones. Your customers can see better than ever before how you treat your employees, which can attract or repel them from your business. Indeed, many companies use their internal culture and teams to promote their products, which can backfire if the company's leadership (i.e., you) fails to follow through on promises to your team. Your shareholders can see how you work with influencers since they are a public-facing group, and that can drive their decision to invest more or less into your company. All of these groups, including, but not limited to, your customers, contribute directly to your traction and growth.

Don't let this expansive definition of your audience overwhelm you, but also don't neglect its influence and power. Let it motivate you and drive your marketing strategy in improved and more effective ways. If we return to the previous example of CEOs using their power and position to behave unbefitting of a leader, we see how, despite it involving an internal group of people and employees, the behavior eventually became transparent. You can never assume things you do will remain under wraps, because I guarantee you people will find out. Do things right and do them well, be open about it, and take care of your entire audience. That's as simple as it needs to be.

Understanding what people want puts you in a much better position to prepare yourself mentally to compete and to give it to them in a way that keeps them coming back for more.

Now we can segment this audience and make the most of each of these relationships. Let's bring this back to your "customer-first" business.

Segmentation Is Not a Bad Word

Your customers have many wants and needs and an almost infinite selection to choose from for how to meet those wants and needs. Targeting an overly broad audience is a poor strategy for gaining business in a crowded marketplace. You must zoom in on subdivisions of customer groups to better understand their unique needs and position yourself as their best possible option. Don't be afraid of losing customers by getting really, *really* specific. Be afraid of weakening your impact on potential customers by not being specific enough.

We all know there are many ways to segment your customer: demographically, geographically, psychographically, and behaviorally are just some of the traditional ones. You might be thinking,

Do I have to? Yes, you do. It might seem old-school, but it works for a reason. Segmenting your customers allows you to meet their unique and specific needs, something you cannot find without going into the nitty-gritty of their lives. It helps you accomplish a couple of things—tailor and personalize your content to resonate with them, adjust your marketing and campaigns to be more effective, create better customer service experiences, and discover new opportunities—all helping you establish customer loyalty.[4]

Precisely Defining Your Target Customers

As an innovation leader, you've likely worked closely with the rest of your team to really get to know your potential customers.

If you're nodding along here and this sounds familiar—great! Identification and segmentation of your target customers are important first steps in your marketing strategy. If your immediate reaction to the previous paragraph was something more along the lines of, *Our market is $100 billion! Everyone is our target customer!*, then you are in trouble. If you aim at every target, you will likely miss them all.

Why do we call them target customers? What is a target customer? Target customers are defined groups of people, and to reach them, you must act *purposefully* and with precise aim.

If you don't know where your target is, you can't hit it with any accuracy. And if you believe that the target is everywhere, you can't act with purpose. It is extremely important to prioritize your target customers. It's similar to darts, and even if you've never played, you most likely know that players aim to hit the bull's-eye in the middle of the board. Think of your marketing strategy as your darts. You have a finite number of darts, and your goal is to use those limited resources to earn as many points as possible during your turn. The more strategic you are about where you aim and the more purposeful you are about how you throw, the more likely you are to crush your competition.

Your Customer Isn't You

Let's say you start a company to solve a problem that you deal with in your own life, either personally or in the industry you're a part of. You saw an opportunity to disrupt a vertical or provide an innovative solution that no one else is doing. I get it. I've done that. But before you get ahead of yourself, don't forget—your customers aren't you.

I train for triathlons, so living an active and healthy lifestyle is extremely important to me. So let's imagine I started a commercial packaged goods (CPG) company around a line of healthy, ready-made foods. As I figure out my marketing strategy, I define my target customers as "men and women who buy groceries."

You should be hearing alarm bells right now. This target is way too broad and entirely reliant on my own personal needs. If I stopped there, I'd be aiming at a huge percentage of the population and competing against all the other companies in this space, from superstore chains like Sam's Club to a weekend farmers market. My darts would be flying every which way. I'd be thinking too many steps ahead: *I buy groceries, and I plan to sell my product in grocery stores, so my target customer is anyone in that grocery store.* I could narrow it down further to men and women who buy organic groceries and live healthfully. I buy organic groceries, and I live healthfully, and if I saw my product on the shelves, I would totally buy it.

But would I? What really motivates me to choose one protein bar over another? Which criteria do I use when deciding which brand of supplements to buy? Does everyone I know—everyone that I have lumped into the category of "target customer that is just like me"—eat the same protein bars and use the same supplements? Probably not. What drives *their* decision-making? That is the type of necessary research that many founders do not conduct because they believe that, in understanding themselves, they already understand everything about their target customer.

The trap here is believing that there are plenty of people like you who have this same problem and want to solve it in the same way—with your product.

Your Target Customer Is *Not* Everyone

Several years ago, I was on a project with a wellness startup that had a great idea for online-only programs. They already had some great content and were almost ready to launch. As we were discussing their marketing rollout plan, I asked them who their initial target customer was.

"Well, it's for everyone who wants to get fit!" one of the founders replied. "Everyone will benefit from our content."

I tried to explain that "everyone" is not a target audience. Fitness and wellness are very large markets with many segments. My team and I tried to use ourselves to illustrate: "Well, I'm training for a triathlon, Letitia goes to the gym once every two weeks, and Charlotte never leaves her couch. Tell me how your content is relevant to each of those three."

As we dug into the content, it became apparent that it was not geared toward fitness novices. The target customer was more like me than like any of the others. We spent a week drilling into what they needed to do to reach that kind of customer and created a well-defined go-to-market plan based on that customer segment.

Now I'll use a real-world example from my own experience at General Assembly[5] (often called GA on Twitter and in the startup community). For those handful of you who may not know, GA is a highly acclaimed private institute that trains business professionals in technology and entrepreneurial skills that they'll need as they grow and manage their businesses.

The highlight reel of the GA story goes something like this: One of its founders, Brad Hargreaves, has a problem. His friends have the same problem, so he decides to build a company for people like him and starts an invite-only coworking space for entrepreneurs.

It's worth noting here that the invite-only model was not put in place to gatekeep the membership and drive demand for an exclusive product but was used by Brad to self-select like-minded people whom he particularly wanted in the workspace. These early members—both people like Brad and people Brad wanted to be like—were chosen for Brad to learn from and thus improve his chances for success.

As that group grew, Brad learned that this community of entrepreneurs needed a lot of help with many aspects of starting a company and that there was an opportunity there for them to help each other out. So Brad started to organize classes around these gaps in knowledge and used those findings to validate educational programming for the startup space. This coincided with a boom in entrepreneurship; suddenly there was a sizable market for educational tools around entrepreneurship and from unlikely sources.

Aspiring founders came from various backgrounds with different needs for their businesses, including wanting to bring cutting-edge digital and tech practices into their large organizations. He expanded his original customer base to include corporate education and training programs and thus capitalized on the deeper pockets of large companies. As Brad learned more about his growing customer base, the company added more offerings to serve career changers and people looking to grow their skill set to gain digital and tech relevance. This eventually resulted in a massive scale-up of the company and a $450 million exit.

Did Brad just have such a great idea that he magically turned it into a thriving company? Spoiler alert: That wasn't it. Did he start by imagining a multimillion-dollar exit and work backward? That never works. Brad started it all by listening to a small, specific group of people in his early customer segment and scaling upward from there to adjacent customer segments and use cases.

Instead of rushing right into opening GA, he agreed to be the entrepreneur-in-residence for a serial founder who was well connected and wanted to create a physical space for other serial founders who were working on new ventures.

When it came to GA, he focused primarily on the audience segment of serial or connected founders to ensure that they were passionate about a supportive entrepreneurship community. Once he mastered that, he expanded his target to include other audience segments that wanted access to tech startup know-how and bridged the gaps between segments by leveraging his existing passionate customers who wanted to share their experience and learn with friends or get their companies to pay for a course or a custom training—an expensive one, not just the starter classes or workshops. One led to more, and he did not try to address all of them at once.

I share all this backstory because, before there was GA's first customer, there were multiple audiences that led to not just the insights for GA or its first members but all of the different audiences that it would take to make it successful. In short, getting specific gets you closer to your target customers. It will also inform decisions about communities and media outlets to engage with and marketing content (what is interesting to this specific audience?). Ultimately, this will give you a far greater chance of reaching people who are the optimal consumers of your product or service. This is also how you begin to define segments within your target audience.

Community

I've always approached building an audience through the lens of community. There are differences between audience and community; traditionally, audience involves things like customer segmentation, for example. Community, on the other hand, includes not just the shared need of the customer but also the shared values of the consumer. If I'm working with a diaper brand, for example, we may be focused on customers who have a need for diapers—duh. But if the company also has a commitment to sustainability, that means that our community is much more complex than just those who need diapers right now. So I might focus my initial audience efforts on attracting those with both an immediate need for diapers and a commitment to the values of sustainability. Don't get me wrong, we still want to sell diapers to anyone who needs them, but our audience is a community that shares the values as well as the need.

If you don't yet realize that segmenting your audience into people of shared values, interests, and behaviors gives way to community, then I've failed in my audience chapter, and I'm retiring early. But assuming you've followed along so far, these indirect communities aren't fully formed yet and need to be captured and enhanced by you. While there may not be a single, recognizable line item that captures the value of community on the balance sheet, that doesn't mean successful communities do not have business value.

Strong communities are valuable to a company in at least three major ways:

- They enhance the value of the brand, which, in turn, drives sales.
- They provide valuable insights into new products and market opportunities.
- They give feedback on products, services, and initiatives, helping optimize investment decisions.

Because communities encourage deeper relationships and create a higher level of trust, they allow organizations to reward based on engagement. For these reasons and more, communities help companies achieve their goals more effectively than potential efficiencies they could achieve with transactional methods.

"So, Lauren," I can hear you asking, "do you really do any of these things yourself?"

Funny you should ask, my friend. Let's talk about how I wrote this chapter. I had a fair idea about the target audience for this book and what my approach should be. But it never hurts to check yourself, so I asked my team and some current startups and former clients to join me in an assumption mapping exercise.

I was surprised by how my perceptions of my audience stacked up when they were challenged by other professionals. Even though I thought I knew who the audience was, I was still surprised by some of the insights that emerged from the exercise. I had to expand my idea of what my audience looked like and what they wanted to hear from me.

And Finally . . .

This won't be the first or last time you hear me harp on the importance of pulling the lens back and making sure you're thoughtfully thinking about creating connection and delivering value to all of your audiences. But it is the first section of strategy because it should absolutely be the foundation from which you build everything in your company. Period. End of story!

Kevin at Big Brand

Kevin is feeling really good as the team finishes up an assumption mapping exercise. They've questioned a lot of the assumptions they had made individually and collectively about what innovation looks like in Big Brand's corporate culture and what it takes to deliver innovation to their customers.

Kevin senses that the team has a better grasp of what they can deliver and how fast they can make it happen, but the question of what they *should* be working on remains. Sitting in his office, he thinks back to business school and remembers a class focused on the JTBD framework. JTBD exercises laser focus on customer needs, and Kevin thinks that will help the team answer the questions: "Why will the customer be interested in Big Brand's innovation? How does it help them?"

At the next team meeting, he's excited to discuss JTBD with the team. He thinks this is going to get them to the next stage of development.

continued

The team listens to his description of how the framework will help and what it entails. Tiff and Aria trade glances, and suddenly Aria raises her hand.

"Kevin, this sounds great, but don't we have to define the customer before we figure out what their need is? I mean, we just did all that assumption mapping, which challenged who we thought we were building for. But we still don't have a clear idea of our actual target audience."

Tiff jumps in. "Aria and I were talking about doing some persona-mapping based on some of our assumption mapping outcomes. Once we have identified a target audience, then we can get down to figuring out what their needs are based on JTBD. Make sense?"

"But won't this take forever?" Kevin asks. "We need to get going, and I think JTBD will get us there faster."

Tiff clears her throat. "Look, Kevin, we can't decide what customers need if we don't have a clear idea of who the customers are. We've been down this road before, and it's not a question of whether the framework is better or faster. They each give you different valuable information that helps create better products."

Aria says, "There's actually something called a ten-minute, persona-mapping workshop. This will help visualize the needs of different customer segments and decide which to focus on with a JTBD exercise. It's a quick and cost-effective solution. Not to mention we have the advantage of working with existing data and insights from Big Brand."

Kevin is surprised at how well the persona-mapping exercises work with the JTBD framework—and it was fast.

They now have documented assumptions mapped and visualized to work off. But at the end of the day, he has a specific target customer and insights into the customer needs that the team will use to start product wireframing and prototyping that he can deliver to Meg and the other MDs as targets for the next quarter.

Jamal and Sarah at Struggling Startup

Sarah and Jamal are meeting Johan to get his take on their next steps. They're discussing the results of the team's assumption mapping exercise. They also mention Nik's research on the competitive product that they debriefed Johan about before meeting.

"So, this is very interesting. Is Nik sure that this isn't a competitor to your product? It sounds like it does the same thing. What's the difference?"

"I don't think we have to worry about it," Jamal adds.

"After we finished the assumption, we all took a breath and moved on to a persona-mapping exercise to validate the new assumptions we'd identified," Sarah added.

"You're spending too much time in the weeds," Johan says. "You need to start shipping the product."

"No, we're not in the weeds," Sarah replies. "Far from it. All this work is helping us get to the right customer segment faster."

"It's true," Jamal adds. "The old me would have gotten your call about a competitive product and jumped into panic

continued

mode, adding features and trying to just get something out the door. These exercises made me slow down and think about who our existing and aspirational customers are, and now we need to explore the trade-offs of getting a product out quicker versus taking our time.

"Next, we're going to try a JTBD exercise to determine the needs of that customer to prioritize the product roadmap."

Johan brightens. "I've had other ventures use JTBD. I think they're using that over at Big Brands on some projects, too. Do you think this is going to help you launch the next product? We need to start generating cash flow and figuring out ROI."

Sarah laughs. "Believe me, no one wants us to start making more money than Jamal and me. If we didn't think this work would help us build the right product for our core customer, we wouldn't waste the time. But doing this kind of work is never a waste of time or money."

Jamal and Sarah are relieved. They feel like the team exercises they've done so far have energized the team and aligned them around a target customer and the need that Struggling Startup should fill. Jamal recognizes that he's been too reactive, struggling with information about the competition and allowing feature creep to enter the product development cycle. Both of them see a way forward that will result in closing the next couple of core customers to increase cash flow, shorten development time, and improve profitability.

Chapter 5

Brand

The word *brand* is thrown around a lot these days. You hear "What is your company's brand?" and "What is your personal brand?" and even "Whatever happened to Russell Brand?" (That's a different book.) The first time I heard the word *brand* was as a kid, watching a Western with my dad. Ranchers brand livestock to mark them as their own; the actual design of that brand visually represents their particular farm and is recognized by all other farmers. While livestock branding isn't my go-to reference, it does highlight the foundation of what branding achieves: It creates a representation of who you are, one that is instantly recognized by others.

But what exactly do I mean when I say *brand*? Keep in mind that I didn't say it was only a visual representation. The visual element is often what is remembered, such as Nike's swoosh symbol or Apple's icon with the missing bite. Think of this as the tip of the iceberg; it's essential to create and to make it so distinct that every other person recognizes the brand as yours, but what moves people to action is an entire brand system. That memorable icon is designed to trigger specific thoughts, emotions, and associations in the minds of others. It's the tone of voice you use, the photography style you implement on posters, the color scheme or use of symbols, and the list goes on.

My first piece of advice is to start where you are. You need to be ruthless in your assessment of your product's appeal, your audience, and your capabilities. It doesn't make any sense to make grandiose branding plans if you are short-staffed and underfunded. That's the time to get creative on a budget—guerrilla marketing, community building, etc. You still need to think about how to create a brand identity, though. Your brand should emerge from every step of creation, from the actual product to the team and company you build. On the other hand, if you're a well-funded startup, you should focus on what your end goal is—acquisition, IPO, or building an actual sustainable business.

If you're operating inside an enterprise and trying to start an innovation team, you must assess how the existing brand will work for the products or services you're trying to create. If it helps, where do you fit? If it doesn't work, what can you build that fits within the existing brand guidelines and infrastructure? Or build on it?

I've spoken a lot about my experience with sports and my interest in physical health, but in my more recent years, I've come to appreciate how equally important our mental well-being is. And through this discovery and new awareness, I encountered a lot of varieties of services and products. I love the story of Headspace, a meditation and mindfulness application created by a former Buddhist monk in 2010.[1] If you aren't one of the 62 million current users,[2] you'll probably end up being one of the 722,000 new monthly visitors eventually.[3]

The founders, Andy Puddicombe (the former monk) and Rich Pierson (a former ad agency executive), wanted to create an accessible, easy-to-use meditation service that could fit right in your pocket. Puddicombe has deep domain knowledge, and meditation isn't something he recently discovered; it's a way of life. Pierson's background in advertising gives him expertise in building brands. It's the perfect team.

Rather than adopt the trendy, new-agey approach common to many mindfulness programs, Headspace took a playful approach that still embodied all the concepts and practices of meditation. The team created characters and illustrations instead of the relaxing music and forest scenes we're so used to seeing. Users felt comforted by these characters guiding them through their mindfulness sessions rather than being faced with photorealistic imagery, and this strategy helped Headspace stand out from competitors.

But awesome graphics and a playful approach don't guarantee success. Headspace's agile and rapid responses to global changes and users' changing needs are what make their brand so compelling and successful. It's not static; it's constantly adapting.

This is one of the biggest misunderstandings about brand: that it's a one-and-done proposition, high fives all around. Unfortunately (or fortunately), this is never the case. Like you do with everything that stays relevant in today's business landscape, keep looking for ways to improve or step up your brand game, and the users will recognize your dedication to them and your product.

It's important to define your brand and understand that it is not just a logo and a creative identity. Brand is a force that drives demand, growth, and connection with stakeholders inside and outside the organization.

Why Building a Brand Matters

Building a brand that drives demand is not about your product or your business model; those are important and are addressed in other parts of this book. It's about the connection you create with your target audience and how the story of the brand influences the customer experience, from product to all communication and experience touch points, to make it better and inspire loyalty. It's as simple and powerful as a myth—a clear, compelling story that draws in your audience.

In order to successfully tell that story, a brand should do three things:

- Establish a *connection* with all your audiences.
- Build *credibility* with those audiences.
- Create *clarity* consistently.

Connection: Build a Relationship with Your Customers

You don't just want to sell to your customers, you want a relationship with them. You want them to love you. You want to pull on their heartstrings and engage with them on an emotional level. You want them to be such diehard fans that they sell your product to people like them for you! This isn't just a catchy jingle that will get stuck in their heads.

When startups are talking about this type of relationship, they use terms like *cult-like following* and *obsessed*. When established brands launch new products, they want to leverage the existing loyalty and engagement of the parent brand if possible. Startup ventures can do the same by leveraging the influence of well-known, credible investors, customers, or strategic partners. Multiple approaches, but they all mean the same thing: connection.

Brand connection is driven by purpose, delivery, resonance, and differentiation. People choose brands that they believe are different from others, provided that the difference is meaningful to them.[4] Writer and former dot-com business executive Seth Godin wrote that brand is "the set of expectations, memories, stories, and relationships that, taken together, account for a consumer's decision to choose one product or service over another."[5] For a brand to be perceived as meaningfully different, it must offer a value proposition its competitors do not, and that offer must resonate with customers. That resonance is your connection.

Think about the brands you consistently use and feel loyal to. What made you choose a MacBook? Why does every venture capitalist wear Patagonia vests? It's not just

Brands tell inspirational stories to consumers, and your customers have to want to be a character in your story.

because of the quality of the product or the efficacy of its marketing. It's because of what you believe that particular branded item says about you. Brands tell inspirational stories to consumers, and your customers have to want to be a character in your story. Our own personal sense of identity shows up in the purchases we make—and in the ones we don't. This isn't just about the rise of personal branding, which is a trend that our digital, hybrid-work world will only continue to fuel. It's about each of our needs to express ourselves, to stand out, and to stand behind our beliefs.

SoulCycle is a massively popular company, and I'm willing to bet that when you saw the word *SoulCycle*, you immediately knew what it was and were able to conjure up a mental image of the type of person who loves SoulCycle. That immediate association is evidence of how strong and deliberate their brand is and how connected they are to their customers. Cofounder Julie Rice said at a Google talk, "People didn't come to SoulCycle because they got fit. It was [for] the connection they got in the room."[6] That brand experience and community connection you got in the room was designed intentionally to energize and hook you! It wasn't just about showing off that you got a great workout; it was about showing off that you got a great workout *and* snagged a competitive slot in a class that sold out in minutes and that maybe you were in the same room as Bradley Cooper. SoulCycle says all of that about each customer.

Red Bull is a case study in building a connection with the target audience through clear, consistent messaging. Red Bull is an energy drink. Their initial target audience was carefully defined: "... predominantly between the ages of 18 and 34, both male and female, with an average-to-high income, and with preferences for sports participation or spectatorship."[7] In other words, young, independent professionals with a taste for adventure.

Their tagline, "Red Bull gives you wings," delivers the brand promise succinctly and effectively. Need to power through a late night at the office? Red Bull gives you wings. Need a little more energy for that last downhill ski run of the day? Red Bull gives you wings. Red Bull's messaging is consistent in all their marketing and advertising media: influencers, event sponsorship, Formula 1 racing sponsorship, print and digital channels, and even user-generated content. This is message discipline on steroids, which, in turn, generates unbelievable levels of brand awareness.

Red Bull has moved well beyond its initial target demographic to achieve cultural ubiquity. But it still aligns the brand image and messaging with high-energy digital marketing and more traditional marketing and advertising campaigns that stress a consumer's need for increased energy. No matter what the marketing or advertising channel, whether it's a commercial about getting out of bed or a video of heli-skiing in the Rockies, Red Bull gives you wings.

As markets become more and more crowded, this type of

connection and message consistency are what will keep your product (and your bottom line) thriving. For example, green consumers buy eco-friendly brands because of what they believe it says about them. But how do green consumers decide between eco-friendly brands? Have you heard of millennial-friendly businesses?[8]

As today's generation of consumers become more and more concerned about social and environmental problems and sustainability, how they choose to spend their money on products has moved away from an ignorance-is-bliss mindset to a socially conscious one. Being socially responsible used to be a plus; now it is a must. To give you some more context, there are more than 4,000 certified B corporations. These are businesses that meet high standards of social and environmental performance, accountability, and transparency.[9]

So yes, building a brand nowadays is harder than ever before but is also more valuable when it is successful. This is where the listening and learning parts of audience discovery become crucial. You are having a conversation with your consumers. You, as a consumer, have conversations with the brands you patronize on a regular basis. Think about how you can apply that to your new venture's offering.

Credibility: Deliver Results on Promises

Warren Buffett said that it takes twenty years to build a reputation and five minutes to ruin it. "If you think about that," he said, "you do things differently." Henry Ford said, "You can't build a reputation on what you are going to do." Neither Mr. Buffett nor Mr. Ford could have predicted how prophetic these quotes would become in an age of fake news, cancel culture, and social media. Can you imagine how Henry Ford would react to X (formerly Twitter)?

Brand credibility hinges on the same principle that personal credibility does: being who you say you are and doing what you promise to do. In people, we would call that integrity. It's challenging to talk about strategy when it comes to credibility because those two words together sound disingenuous. A strategy to get people to trust you sounds like you're trying to trick them (or run for office). When I talk about your credibility strategy, I'm talking about the creation and delivery of your values as embodied in the company and brand. This is about delivering on who and what you say you are and doing what you promise to do, just as a person of integrity would.

How can you be true to your brand identity and brand values, and continuously measure yourself against them? How do you communicate who you really are to your customers and how do you consistently show up as the brand your customers believe that you are? It starts with your brand identity.

Brand Identity

Almost every company can be thought of as a person.[10] In the same way that you create profiles of your target customers, your customer creates an idea of the person that your brand embodies. This person is your brand identity. Your brand identity should be relatable to your target customers and should have qualities that your target audience can stand by because, believe it or not, at least 63 percent of potential consumers "prefer to conduct purchases from brands that support a purpose that aligns with their own values," according to Farhat Zishan, who examined Nike's "Dream Crazier" campaign.[11]

Nike is a huge brand known in virtually every corner of the globe at this point. I'm partial to Nike because my first real management job was running one of their concept shops. It was a blast. I learned so much about all of the moving parts that make up a brand, including the importance of specificity in brand identity and the in-person experience that brings it to life. Although the company could have taken the broad tack that everyone wears shoes and that its identity could be shared with anyone, Nike built strong relatability by playing directly to those who identify as athletes and its customers' desires to be an athlete. These aren't shoes for just anyone; they're shoes for elite competitors. That brand identity still attracted weekend road warriors and casual sports players because it appeals to those customers' aspirations. It also allowed Nike to grow from its origins of running sneakers and shorts to equipment and even their digital products like the Nike running app and community.

Nike maintains that credibility by living by its brand DNA; everything the company has done sticks to that original identity. They have set the guardrails on who they are and who they are not, and they aren't afraid to scare off people who are not in their target audience and don't identify with the DNA of their chosen brand identity.

Take their naming Colin Kaepernick as a brand ambassador after he was dropped from the NFL for protesting racial injustice during the national anthem. The NFL was bending to the will of the masses, but Nike stuck by its brand ethos and supported an athlete they admired. Take their polarizing "Dream Crazier" campaign, which ran during the 2019 Academy Awards and addressed the specific challenges faced by female athletes. These decisions were polarizing, but were also on-brand for Nike, and ultimately only intensified the loyalty of their target customers.[12] It created a lot of chatter and offended many, even some of their male customers. But, staying true to their brand image and personality, they stood by their decision and authentic beliefs to deepen their connection with their female athlete community.

Caution!

A word of caution to leaders: Your brand identity is not you, and it should not be you. Steve Jobs became an icon and symbol of Apple, but the company didn't design its brand image around him, and thank God for that. You want the brand legacy and loyalty to extend far beyond you. This doesn't mean that you don't or shouldn't share core beliefs; if you're a startup founder, those beliefs are probably a big part of why you started the company to begin with. If you're a leader at a large company, its existing brand identity was likely a significant factor in why you chose to work there. But brand identity must be bigger than any single person at a company. The founder's personal beliefs—whatever they are—are NOT scalable, and if you want to build a profitable, sustainable, and sellable company, you want it to scale beyond the founder.

Trust

Trust is perhaps the only genuine currency left in the world. When your customers trust you, they'll not only keep coming back to you but will also give you valuable insight into other problems that you can solve for them, which in turn creates more potential relationships and revenue streams with and from them.

Your customers need to trust that you are what you've spent all of this time telling them you are. Remember that your customers believe that your brand says something about them. Wearing those Converse sneakers or a pair of Christian Louboutin heels with their signature red undersoles tells the world something about that person that they want to communicate. It's very personal, which is why a betrayal of that brand is something that your customers can take very personally.

Think of the scandals surrounding Uber, which was plagued with unethical actions and problematic communication from its founders,[13] or Mast Brothers industrial chocolate masquerading as "bean to bar."[14] These breaches of trust are directly related to the specific brand that the company built, which is a much bigger violation in the eyes of your customers. Scandals can often be attributed to bad leadership, which can be replaced and in Uber's case became the solution. But a betrayal of brand identity is connected directly to your product and is much more difficult to overcome.

Your customers are using your product to differentiate themselves. If the message that your brand is sending the world is not what your customer thinks it is, it is treachery—like Brutus betraying Caesar or almost anything Littlefinger did over eight seasons on *Game of Thrones*. It's not necessarily about whether your brand does something wrong, it's about whether what you do violates the belief system you share with your target customers.

Provide Real Value

Building enviable credibility is also dependent on your ability to create value for customers and to be perceived as delivering even more value than expected. I've seen both founders and corporate innovators fall into the trap of competing with *price* instead of with *value*. As leaders, we must ask ourselves, *What value is being created? How is it being delivered? How are we showing up for our customers?* Then, we must communicate those answers to our customers.

Credibility is massively important to your brand. If your customers trust your brand and you keep showing up as the company they believe you are, you'll have them forever.

Clarity: Clear, Consistent Communication of Your Purpose, Promise, and Value

Clarity shows up often in this book because it is both a leadership and performance principle that is crystallized in brand work. All of your company's communication, both internal and external, must be clear, compelling, and consistent so as to gain awareness, traction, and preference—they are required to drive demand. Your outward-facing brand is for the customer experience while the internal brand is often called "employer brand" and is used to recruit talent and essential vendors that help you deliver on your promise.

Clarity starts with your vision. Do you clearly see what your company's brand is? Most leaders are clear on the *what* of their company; clarity requires that you truly understand the *why*. Why your company, why this problem, why this approach, why this solution, and why now? And if you're gunning to build a venture-backed company, investors will ask, *Why you?* Without a why, you won't be able to craft a strong story to sell to your customers. Without a why, whatever your company seeks to accomplish will lack the spark necessary to carry you forward.

That becomes the promise you make about what your company does, what it stands for, who it serves, and the purpose behind your work. Your company's brand will thrive or die on those promises. This is where clarity helps you. Explicitly stating your promises to your stakeholders not only helps them choose you over the competition (that's your future customers, employees, investors, etc.) but also helps you (and your people) know how to make decisions of all sizes and empower your growing team to do so as well because you know what promises you have baked into the brand. These promises are made to guide you. Think of them as brand guardrails.

Where to Begin?

Once again, start where you are. Here are some questions to ask yourself as you begin your brand journey. This does change depending on whether you are a founder or corporate innovator. Feel free to read both sections because you don't know what the future will bring.

As a founder, you should identify the promises you want to make to your customers. Which can you deliver on now? Which are part of the vision but can't be delivered in the short term? Identify the communication channels you will use to clearly and consistently deliver on those promises (and news of the fulfillment of those promises). Make sure that all decision-makers and any employees who might speak publicly about your organization deliver the same message.

Corporate innovators should start with the promises that your established brand has made. What are they? How does your company deliver on them? Are there examples of when those promises were broken, and if so, what was the customer's reaction? That's all great research that will help you understand how to leverage your existing brand. Can your new products or services deliver on those promises? If not, why? Now think about the additional promises that your new product or service is making to its customers. Though you are innovating, they must be compatible with your parent company's promises, especially if you're going to leverage their customer base. How will you or the parent company communicate these promises and their fulfillment both internally and to new and existing customers? Which existing channels can you leverage to promote your new product or service?

Whether you're submerged in the day-to-day madness of running a startup or the mind-boggling minutiae of building something new in a larger company, it's easy to lose sight of the why behind what you are trying to accomplish and who you're trying to serve. A clear, compelling, consistent why keeps you on your path and simplifies decision-making every day. It sets the expectations for what your company will deliver to your team, your customers, your investors, everyone! So be sure to maintain perfect clarity on what those promises are. It's quite easy to overdeliver, and underdelivering will kill you.

And Finally . . .

Building a brand means starting where you are. It's vital to understand what your real value proposition is and how you plan to deliver on that promise. All your communications—to customers, employees, vendors, investors, and other stakeholders—should reinforce your brand message and, therefore, your brand promise. Branding is an ongoing activity. Even if you have a compelling, evergreen message like Red Bull, how and where that message is delivered should be ever evolving.

Effective branding has the power to humanize any company into a persona that audiences can identify with. Craft your brand early and use it intentionally as a tool to drive your company's growth. Keep the three Cs in mind: connection, credibility, and clarity. They represent the fundamental point of a brand that makes it successful. And last, but definitely not least, stay on top of your game. Don't ever finish branding; keep up to date with things and iterate according to your users' needs and the changing landscape just as you would with your product. You won't regret it or the value it adds to your bottom line.

Kevin at Big Brand

In the last team meeting, the brand manager, Rikki, had asked several difficult questions: "So, are the things we're working on part of Big Brand's brand architecture, or are we going in a different direction? Are we building a new brand? Or should we be using Big Brand's assets? Is this initiative a separate entity? If it's a separate thing, what should we be building the brand around?"

Kevin and Rikki agreed that they needed to speak with Sohana, the brand director, so they've called her in. He's also invited Tiff to come along.

"Well, you can't do anything that contradicts what we've already established in our brand guidelines," Sohana says. "This is a well-established company with a global reputation. You can't do anything that puts that in jeopardy."

"Well, wait a second," Tiff interjects. "How can we do something different if it has to follow the same old rules?"

Kevin tries to get Tiff to slow down a second. "We can't just change everything. There will always be rules we have to follow."

"But if we want new results, we have to adapt our way of doing things, right?" Tiff asks.

"Our brand strategy works," Sohana says. "It has evolved with our place in the market."

continued

Kevin speaks up, "I have an idea."

Two weeks later, he finds himself in the largest meeting he's ever hosted. He suggested that they open the question of branding for the innovation initiative to representatives from all over the organization. Tiff got excited right away, and they eventually brought Sohana around to their point of view.

"Okay, we can try this," Sohana says. "But in prepping for the meeting, remember how we view brand-building overall. We're always looking for ways to connect with customers and markets: What are their expectations, pain points, and aspirations? Once you connect, how do you build credibility? What market research, customer access, brand equity, and resources do we already have access to?"

"Yes, we can't forget to leverage our access to Big Brand's resources. We have subject matter experts on payroll; let's utilize them!" Tiff interjects.

Sohana continues after the interruption. "The path to credibility leads through trust, and trust takes time. And patience. And deliberation. It requires constantly reassessing your deliverables and actions considering your promise to your customers. It also means that, in all your communication efforts (PR, advertising, social media, marketing), what you *say* should reflect what you *do* and how you do it.

"All of this grows out of the clarity that you have around your brand identity. It involves clarity of vision, of purpose, of story, of communication. And that is where the real work lies. If you are not clear about what promises you're making, how you achieve them, and how your customers and other stakeholders will benefit, you will never build a successful brand identity."

Kevin turns to the rest of the group. "The goal for today is to run a thirty-minute collaborative ideation workshop, known as How Might We,[15] to come up with ideas on how to brand Big Brand's new innovation initiative. I'm going to turn you over to Tiff to organize into teams and get started. I'd like us to have a strategic direction by the end of the day. We'll worry about tactics later."

Several hours later, the meeting has succeeded beyond Kevin's expectations. The enthusiasm grew throughout the meeting, and everyone was engaged and invested.

What came out of the meeting were two insights: The team is focused on both incremental improvements to existing products and services, as well as the exploration of new opportunities. It was agreed that product improvements would be branded with existing brand guidelines within the product line. A new sub-brand will be created for the opportunities that are uncovered. Sohana's team will be an integral part of building this new brand so that it melds with Big Brand's overall strategy.

Kevin realizes that he's got to refocus on deliverables. But he's still pleased with the way things are coming together.

Jamal and Sarah at Struggling Startup

"But who are you guys, really?"

Sarah is checking in with their customer contact, Omar.

continued

"When I try to explain who you are as a vendor," Omar continues, "I keep falling back on a product description. I know you and Jamal are trying to move beyond that, so what's the story?"

Sarah repeated her conversation with Omar to Jamal; Nik, the product person; and Nina, their head of marketing.

"Well, this is what I've been talking about for nine months," Nina says. "I've told you over and over that we need to work on all the different aspects of brand-building while you're building the product. Great product isn't enough—even in the B2B space."

"We only have one product," Jamal says. "Do we really need branding?"

"Brand isn't just for the big boys," Nina chides. "It's about building identity and community as well. Omar is right. All we really have is a product description and a pitch deck we use along with our sales demo."

"So, what do we do?" Sarah asks. "Remember, we don't have a ton of money for all this."

"And none of us has time to post cute workplace memes," Jamal grumbles.

"Dude," Nik interjects, "so not the point. Nina's right. You hired me to shepherd products to market. We've identified the market and we have a couple customers, but we really haven't focused on our identity in that market to attract more and how to build an effective message around that identity."

"Exactly right, Nik!" Nina exclaims. "We still haven't planted our flag, clearly differentiated ourselves, or built a solid community around what we're trying to achieve. And,

Jamal, I'm not talking about memes. That's a tactic; I'm talking strategy and a story."

"So, what do we have to do?" Sarah asks, giving Jamal a look.

"Well, first, I think we need to get the whole team aligned on what our identity is," Nina replies.

"Ooh, ooh!" Sarah exclaims. "I was just at a conference, and one of the workshops introduced us to the Team Canvas template. It helps teams align around different goals. We could use it to help us align on brand identity and message!"

"I've heard about it," Nina says. "It's a short exercise and gives us a physical representation about what alignment looks like. I love it. If you want, I can set up that meeting right away."

"Sounds good," Nik says, "but first, you two need to have a serious conversation about what you think the company's identity really is. That way, you can provide the team with some guidelines to start the alignment process. It will also help us. I love you two, but sometimes you're all over the place."

"Once we've settled on an identity and message," Nina adds, "then we can get down to the tactics that will create an impact with our audience and build momentum for our product launches."

The workshop is a real eye-opener for Jamal and Sarah.

"I guess we weren't as aligned as we thought we were," Jamal muses. "Everyone seemed pretty confused at the beginning. It took a little longer than I thought it would, but I realize that's down to us . . . It's so clear in my mind."

continued

"For me, too! We have got to get better at solidifying this kind of clarity with the team," Sarah says. "For them to effectively embody our identity and help our customers do the same, we need to be clear on what we expect them to talk to us about."

But Nina and Nik seemed pleased. Nina says now she's got the foundation for decent brand strategy, and we'll have the first pass next week to react to and start testing in the market.

"I've never seen Nik look so relieved," Jamal adds.

"I feel like we're starting to finally move ahead."

Chapter 6

Category

The concept of category is a strategic approach to your company's business landscape. I also refer to it as your *competitive ecosystem*. It helps companies create, develop, and dominate existing categories and create new categories of products and services instead of focusing only on beating the other guy, which is ultimately only a short-term game. Category aligns much better than a simplistic focus on competition, with the strategy, prototyping, and validation work that goes into building a new venture in the digital world. Think of a swim meet, with a pool full of swimmers straining inch by inch, focused on breaking their own personal bests in every heat, all trying to win; that's your competition.

But focusing only on the competition leaves too many opportunities on the table. Category starts with the consumer, not the competition. This is a radical shift for a lot of businesses. They tend to view their products and services in the ecosystem of other businesses. But shifting the perspective to the consumer shows how

expansive the competitive ecosystem actually is, involving more
than just similar products and
services. It's also about expanding

Category starts with the consumer, not the competition.

your perception of value-creation, considering the unmet customer
needs (that they may not even be aware of yet), and giving any
business a competitive advantage. But it means expanding your perspective and welcoming new challenges, as well as ways of creating
or delivering value.

For example, think about the rise of the meal kit industry.
Cooking used to involve finding a recipe, grocery shopping, measuring, and waste. (I only need a pinch of nutmeg. What am I going
to do with the other three ounces? And how big is a pinch anyway?)
Many young Americans (and older ones, frankly) had never been
taught to cook a meal. They had cookbooks and cooking shows, but
they never learned how to put together a full meal for themselves.

Companies like Blue Apron and HelloFresh have redefined the
category of home cooking. They deliver to the home all pre-por-
tioned ingredients for either single or family meals, which the
consumer prepares. It eliminates shopping, measuring, and food
waste. People knew they hated wasting food, that grocery shopping
was a pain, and that they didn't really understand all the measurements in recipes, but they didn't know that they wanted a meal kit
delivered with fresh ingredients.

HelloFresh entered the market in 2012 and invested in extolling
the virtues of home cooking. They demonstrated how their product
makes it a fun, fast experience. They recognized that their competition wasn't other home cooking products but frozen meals,
restaurants, and meal delivery.

The US meal kit industry was worth $15.21 billion in 2021.
What began as a disruptive force is now an established category,

attracting giants like Amazon. Meal kits reached $20.5 billion in 2022.[1] These companies created a new category in the food industry.

Category is not a new concept; it's how humans have always organized the information around them. Consumers categorize products based on their perceived needs. The way we approach category design is by helping them identify the needs they aren't aware of yet.

Category Design

Since 2012, category design has emerged as the discipline of analysis and strategy, with the end goal of creating and monetizing new markets in a massively noisy world. It's about establishing your own niche by educating customers in a market to think about a problem and its solution in the way you want them to.

There are different approaches to category design. The book *Play Bigger* analyzes some of Silicon Valley's biggest success stories (Amazon, Salesforce, IKEA), companies that have changed our perceptions of what we need, when we need it, and how we need to get it.[2] Al Ramadan and his coauthors dubbed these companies the *category kings*. They outline a playbook that every founder and innovator should consult before they embark on creating a new product or service. Here's a summary of the questions from the playbook:

- What's missing in the marketplace?
- What is the descriptive name for this?
- Who else should we be working with?
- How do we frame our unique solution?

- How do we own the key control points?
- How do we change how people think?
- How do we build momentum?

I think these are important questions that any leader needs to ask before they start a new project. What the consumer needs is more important than what you want to build. And if your product or service is not aligned with an existing need or a new one you've identified, then your efforts will fail.

So how do you identify what the consumer really needs, you ask? Well, for that we need to take a brief (and I do mean brief) dip into behavioral psychology. If you've ever read work on cognitive biases, like Daniel Kahneman's book *Thinking, Fast and Slow*,[3] you will recognize how these concepts tie into the behavioral patterns of the human brain. Good category design plays right into cognitive biases like the choice supportive bias and the groupthink bias. This doesn't mean that you're tricking people! It just means that you're adapting your company's approach to the way that people—your customers—already think and behave so you all win.

Discovering and designing a category problem—the first question on our list—is part of disruption and innovation. You've heard those words a million times by now, so we won't belabor *disruption* here. But I want to highlight an often-overlooked part of disruption and innovation, which is a deep understanding of *unmet needs* and *untapped desires*. While those sound like two installments in a romance novel franchise, they're actually the most important parts of innovation. But like a romance novel, you need to think about how consumers will react emotionally to your idea. How does this make my life better or easier? Does it make me smarter, sexier? How does it make me feel?

You'll notice that the questions listed earlier aren't just about how to create your new product; you also have to sell it. And selling it requires convincing consumers that the new product or service will indeed make them smarter or sexier or make their life better or easier. This is why the concept of category is so important. I've seen a lot of startups and innovation labs come up with brilliant, game-changing products or services. But they couldn't convince anyone that they needed it—and so they failed.

All of this is to say that defining a category, creating a clear story, and then mobilizing and shaping your customers' thinking around the need you've identified is essential to a successful endeavor.

Business Model

This approach is an ongoing process in both category strategy and your business model. Given that category design often includes changing the business model or how value is delivered, it's relevant that, to create or disrupt a category, you must look critically at the business model. As you consistently evaluate your category (externally), it's also important to innovate your business model to keep up with—or preferably overtake—your competition. Think about what happened to Blockbuster after Netflix emerged. And then think about how Netflix evolved when cable companies began offering instant downloads of movies (does anyone even get the DVDs anymore?). And then think about the original programming race that Netflix and others in its category—Amazon Prime, Hulu, YouTube, and now Apple—are currently engaged in.

I really like the Business Model Canvas for this type of analysis. It's a strategic management and lean startup template for developing new businesses, envisioning new possibilities for existing businesses that need to reinvent, or documenting existing business models. Its one-page format captures and describes the company's value proposition (more on that to follow), including infrastructure, customers, and finances.[4] Figure 6.1 is an example, and I highly recommend digging into Alexander Osterwald's original 2008 work and the niche offshoots for user experience, internal communications, etc. You can find a variety of examples and applications on the Strategyzer website.

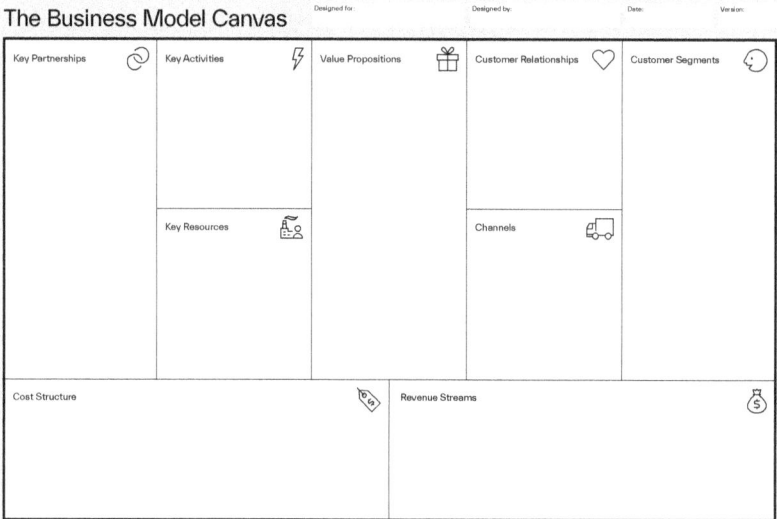

The Business Model Canvas

Key Partnerships	Key Activities	Value Propositions	Customer Relationships	Customer Segments
	Key Resources		Channels	

Cost Structure		Revenue Streams	

Figure 6.1. The Business Model Canvas ©2020 Strategyzer AG strategyzer.com

Situational Awareness

To figure out your plan of action, you need to develop situational awareness. Having strong situational awareness helps you carve out your place in your category and maintain your edge as the market evolves. Most innovators' situational awareness is not as sharp as they think it is. They think they've seen it all, but they haven't. They rely too much on assumptions, which is always a dangerous move.

Or they take a good look around and then stop paying close attention, which means they miss out on changes in their category.

Situational awareness is not a one-and-done approach in which you only look at the landscape when you're putting together a pitch deck; it must be an ongoing process to make sure that no one is coming to eat your lunch! The market changes, technology changes, customers' preferences and behaviors change. Maintaining strong, ongoing situational awareness is a key part of understanding your audience, achieving product–market fit, and informing new features and trends to stay competitive. I cannot stress enough how important this is to your company's success in your chosen category.

To develop situational awareness, first assess the entirety of your category, analyze the position of the players, and then build your strategy. Let's practice with one of the first startups I got to work with as they were scaling up: Crunch Fitness.

Crunch started in the late 1980s, hosting in-person and cable TV group exercise classes, as well as producing DVD instruction. After a private equity (PE) buyout, it evolved into one of the fastest-growing franchise fitness companies in the world. In addition to in-person group classes, they also offer personal training, functional group training, apparel and other merchandise, and in some locations, food and beverages. Their newest offering is Crunch Plus, an exercise-streaming platform that includes customizable workout plans, virtual personal training, unlimited access, and more.[5]

What is Crunch's category? Did you say gyms? Nope. That is a shortsighted assessment and will yield poor situational awareness. Crunch's category is the *entire* health and fitness industry. This includes gyms, which is Crunch's direct business competition, and studios devoted to specific exercise regimes (Pilates, yoga, etc.), and also includes health food and vitamin stores such as GNC and The Vitamin Shoppe; apparel companies like Nike and Lululemon;

and specialty fitness equipment like Peloton. It also includes indirect competition alternatives like Juice Press, Bulletproof, and even WeightWatchers. In today's world, you're competing on share of wallet, attention, and all of the potential alternatives to the outcome your customer is looking for. Crunch needs to assess all of those parts of the fitness category. To focus on just what other gyms are doing would be shortsighted and dangerous for Crunch, because it wouldn't include everything happening in their category.

Assess your world in detail. Analysis of the category landscape helps innovation leaders select points of focus and identify the patterns of behavior that drive interactions and thus drive revenue. Let's stay with our fitness landscape but consider another player: Peloton. I briefly mentioned how they are in competition with Crunch, despite delivering very different physical products. But they happen to be an interesting example to demonstrate how important it is to constantly be analyzing the landscape and keeping up with changes.

The COVID-19 pandemic limited the use of traditional gyms and participating in outdoor activities, but, like Netflix and Nintendo, Peloton's offering and business model was uniquely suited to the pandemic environment. As gyms closed their doors and scrambled to find alternative revenue models to ride out the pandemic, Peloton became an impulse purchase for many consumers as they struggled to find ways to keep fit while confined to their homes. Revenue skyrocketed; it doubled in 2020 and again in 2021 as Peloton expanded its capacity, but not necessarily its offering.[6] However, as new competitors emerged in the virtual training space (many without expensive hardware requirements) and physical workout locations slowly reopened, Peloton's revenue growth and customer base expansion evaporated.

Instead of capitalizing on the explosive growth they experienced in order to expand their category offerings—for example, into branded physical locations like SoulCycle—Peloton seemed to be content to ride the wave until it crashed. Peloton created an abrupt shift in the competitive landscape but failed to continuously monitor the situational landscape and continuously adapt. Change is never one-and-done. Innovation and disruption are constants, whether it's an expansion during an unprecedented event or the inevitable recovery and return to business as usual.

Consider your *direct competition*—the products and services that are similar to yours in multiple ways—even if they don't compete with the same additional services or functionality. Also consider your *indirect competition*—products and services that are different but intended to solve the same problem and are thus substitute offerings that your customer could choose instead of your product. Companies need to be strategic in how they think about their category in order to enhance innovation and have a crystal-clear understanding of their customers' options.

As you analyze your direct competition, look for the following competitive factors:

- The number of competitors, a.k.a. market saturation
- The qualitative differences between you
- Any other differences in your product or offering
- The level of customer loyalty that others have
- The cost to the customer to switch to your product or service

When you look at your indirect competition, consider the following:

- The availability of different solutions addressing the same customer need or pain point

- The cost to the customer to switch to your product or service
- The price–performance trade-offs of these substitutes

Finally, study the future of the competitive rivalry in your category. Ask yourself these questions:

- What is the market trend? Growth or decline?
- What are the barriers to enter the market (regulations, patents, specific expertise, high amount of capital to start, etc.)?
- Which innovations can change the landscape?

Performing this competitive analysis helps to develop your category strategy—the points of differentiation, advantages, and an action plan to stand out from the crowd of rivals. It also gives you much better situational awareness, which puts you in a better position when an unanticipated threat—like, say, a global pandemic—strikes.

If you're anything like me, your wallet or phone is often backed with different fitness class cards (gym, yoga, Pilates), as well as schedules for different classes and teachers. Finding a class can be tedious and time-consuming; that's why ClassPass changed my life. Suddenly, I had access to a wide range of fitness classes all over my city without having to join multiple studios. It was great!

Its founder, Payal Kadakia, was a dancer, someone who enjoyed various types of classes and looked forward to trying them at different studios. However, finding classes that suited her dance style, schedule, and location as a former consultant quickly became problematic. Kadakia recalled that, one night, she completely missed a lesson by being bogged down in her research on upcoming class types and instructor specifics. If she had this much difficulty, so must others. The need was there, and so the idea was born—a purely subscription-based model. It wasn't successful right away. Originally named Classtivity, it was an online thirty-day pass that could be used at any partner fitness facilities. She found that her audience was reluctant to register online and try new classes. Kadakia understood this resistance, and rather than continue to push her idea onto unwilling customers, she found the potential for a new niche.

The business model was revamped, and in 2014, Classtivity was rebranded as ClassPass.[7] It uses a subscription-based model where members can go online and book classes with various studios and is modeled after OpenTable. Members pay a $99 monthly fee, similar to a gym or single studio membership, and have different class types to choose from without being tied to a single studio. This did several things for the company. First, its brand promise and value proposition were simplified: ClassPass is an easy way to find and reserve a spot at a favored facility. Second, the brand was becoming known as a reliable platform and created an economical and easy way to gain variety in health and fitness (a byproduct of business model design). And finally, the unlimited number of classes a member could take, similar to a gym or a studio, maximized the value of the pass by reserving favorite workouts while giving users the flexibility of trying new activities for one low monthly fee similar to the gym or studio they'd be switching from. And switch they did!

In 2020, ClassPass was considered a unicorn—being valued at over $1 billion before going public. And the pandemic didn't stop Kadakia. As studios and classes were canceled during lockdown, the studios used their existing limited supply and virtual products and brought them to the forefront of ClassPass. Their digital library of video-on-demand classes became a lifeline not only for ClassPass but for the partnered studios that now had no other way of staying open and generating cash flow. In 2021, ClassPass was acquired by MindBody, the leading health and wellness technology platform.[8]

Payal Kadakia noticed a problem that she had, figured out that others were dealing with the same problem (even though they couldn't really explain it), and created a service that solved the problem and acquired millions of devoted customers in the process. That, my friends, is category.

And Finally . . .

I want to stress that category is an ongoing process. Too many entrepreneurs and innovators settle for finding initial success in a category and never moving beyond that. You should ask yourself the following questions:

- Are my direct competitors still the same?
- Are there new areas of indirect competition?
- Is my whole market expanding or contracting?
- Where is my company in that cycle?
- Are there other business model innovations or interrupts that would allow me to capture value and, therefore, a competitive edge?

These are just a few of the questions that I make it a point to examine regularly for both my own business and those who rely on my expertise. Remember, defining a category is the first step. You still have to be on the lookout for ways to expand your initial category offerings and seek new opportunities in the marketplace. The category approach allows you to consider all your options and figure out how to thrive in crowded markets.

Kevin at Big Brand

After the success of the brand exercises, Sohana suggested they begin holding monthly meetings. Tiff and Kevin are preparing for today's meeting.

"A lot of the managers and MDs really like these get-togethers," Tiff says. "They get the chance to be more hands-on and contribute to the future of the organization during these workshops."

"Well, it's great for us," Kevin replies. "It gets us a lot of upfront buy-in on the decisions we're making. Plus, they all feel like they're invested in our success."

"So what's the story with this 'category' idea?" Tiff asks.

Kevin smiles. "Sohana walked me through it the other day, and it makes so much sense. Basically, it's a different way for us to analyze the marketplace and our competition. It helps us identify places where our innovation efforts will have the best opportunity for Big Brand to win."

"Isn't that just the competitive landscape?" Tiff asks.

"Not really," Kevin replies. "It's not just about existing direct competition but also indirect competition, customer demographics, new technologies, new delivery methods, and finding new customer needs that they don't know they have."

"That's a lot," Tiff says. "How are we going to accomplish that in just a couple of hours?"

continued

"That's why Sohana wanted to get everybody together again," Kevin says. "Let's stop by her office right now and go over some of this."

"What's up?" Sohana asks when they knock on the door.

"I was explaining category to Tiff ahead of this meeting, and she had some questions," Kevin replies.

"Great! Fire away," Sohana says.

"Well, first, we know our competition; why is it important to think about this?" Tiff asks.

Sohana replies, "It seemed like a good idea to get input from a range of perspectives inside the company. In your innovation effort, it makes sense to view it through the lens of category when it comes to Big Brand's present and especially future landscape."

"Why?" Tiff asks.

"Look," Sohana says, "Big Brand absolutely rules in some categories, like our fitness apparel division. But we don't want to be Marriott and dismiss an opportunity like Airbnb and then be a late mover after we've lost share of wallet."

"Oh. Yesss," Tiff says. "I understand. Definitely don't want to miss the boat."

"Since innovation is about disruption, I don't think you want to start by disrupting a category that Big Brand leads. It makes more sense to find a category that hasn't been developed or one that is ripe for disruption where we don't have as much of a presence. Does that make sense?" Sohana proposes.

Tiff puzzles, "But how does that actually help us figure out what to do?"

"The people we've gathered will help us figure out what

categories the company already has the capability to disrupt—one where we're not a leader but have a presence," Kevin answers.

"Exactly," Sohana says. "There are a series of questions that we're going to workshop at the meeting. We have to start by identifying categories that we don't own that are ripe for disruption. Then we ask, *What is there an abundance of, and what are the customers asking for? What new solutions and value can we bring?* From there, we'll take what we find and build off it, identifying the name of our category position and then who we need to reach out to.

"I've sent both of you a list of all the questions we should answer. I don't expect to get to all of them. Kevin, what do you want to get out of this meeting?"

"If we can figure out one or two categories by the end of the session that we could focus discovery on, with maybe some ideas about possible problems customers are facing, that would be ideal," Kevin answers. "Then the team and I can dig in with the various functional teams to refine the problem definition and figure out if we have the resources to tackle a solution."

Tiff nods. "It's really clear when you lay it out this way."

"I knew you'd get there," Sohana laughs. "See you Monday."

Jamal and Sarah at Struggling Startup

Jamal and Sarah are talking with Nik and Nina, the marketing director, about the branding exercise Nik's team ran.

continued

"So, we have a pretty clear idea of where we need to take this," Sarah says. "We're finally aligned on what the company stands for and what we want to project to our customers."

"It's nice that you know what to tell the customers," Nina says, "but have we actually defined who the customers are?"

"Excellent point, Nina," Alex interjects. "One of the things I realized during the workshop is that you need to better understand your market and your place in it."

"We know who our biggest customer is. Just look for more customers like that," Jamal replies.

"That's a recipe for disaster," Nina says. "They're our customer because of your personal connection. More customers *like that* are impossible to identify."

"Nina's right," Alex says. "You're making way too many assumptions about your market and the competitive landscape. Are you familiar with the concept of category?"

"Oh, yes!" Nina exclaims. "I've been trying to get them to understand how we need to approach the market. This is perfect."

"What are you two talking about?" Jamal is confused and annoyed.

"I know you know about the competitive landscape," Alex says. "But competition is really more of an ecosystem—not only direct competition but indirect competition and dependencies. You need to clearly define where you want to fit in that ecosystem and then build a strategy that reflects that."

"Yeah," Nina says. "You just keep thinking about the next step, the next customer, the next sale. Category lets you plan not just your next step but several steps ahead."

"But our customer is really happy with the product," Sarah says.

"Sure, your customer is a good fit," Alex explains. "But you have to understand whether you can also fill the need for other companies—at a scale that will make your organization profitable."

"I thought we really understood the market," Jamal says.

"Look, *market* is really broad," Alex says. "You have to clarify why a customer should buy your product. Have you identified a new need that they have? Do they understand how your product helps them?"

"Our messaging strategy doesn't really define any of that," Nina says. "Whether it's doing something better or doing something new, how is what we sell the solution?"

"So how do we answer that?" Jamal asks.

Nina looks at Alex. "What about filling out a Business Model Canvas?"

Alex nods. "That gives you a template to analyze your current model and helps you figure out what you might be able to exploit profitably. The canvas makes you look critically at your place in the market and where you want to go."

Nina opens a version of the canvas on her laptop and shows Sarah and Jamal.

"I can do some research on the competitive landscape to help fill it out," Nina says. "We can do one together if you like. Maybe Alex will stick around?"

"I think we should fill one out, then create another with your team," Alex says. "I think you'll be surprised by the gap between your answers and the team's."

continued

"Okay," Jamal says. "Send us some links about the canvas and how other companies have used it. We'll schedule a meeting for the four of us and then another meeting with the whole team."

"I think we should send a copy of the template to the team beforehand," Nina says. "They may each want to start filling it out before the meeting."

Sarah grins. "Sometimes I wonder what we've gotten ourselves into."

Part 3

Operations

*C*hange is the only constant. That's a message I've been sharing for over a decade, and the world continues to remind us of the truth in it. Your context will change; the world will change. This business you have today is not the business you had yesterday or the one you'll have tomorrow. Thinking like a brand but acting like a startup will help you prepare for the changes and stay grounded in times of chaos by focusing on what delivers value and examining the assumptions you make about it. And if you become adept at both having the mindset and living in the tension and duality of the two, you likely will be able to consistently thrive while riding the waves, whether you face calm waters or turbulent seas.

I've thrown a couple of models at you so far, but the one I'm about to introduce is different. *Think Like a Brand. Act Like a Startup.* encourages you to integrate a new operating model with your existing ways of work (Agile, Scrum, Kanban, etc.). It is flexible enough for you to bring new things or players into your way of work, whereas other operating models are known for being more rigid in their approach. I understand that work and business do not take place in a vacuum, and I fully expect that this model will be used in a highly individualized context. After working intimately with hundreds of startups over the last decade in countless different environments, industries, stages, and business models, and running one of the largest startup portfolios in the world, I know firsthand that there is an exception to every rule and that frameworks are there for structure and guidance, not to hamstring you with rigidity. Any that do that, don't serve the true essence of innovation.

When I use this in my own startup portfolio, ventures, or former consulting business, I leverage the approach and framework but customize it each time. The operating model is here to give you guardrails and help create clarity, which can result in throughput and momentum to achieve your goals. It's flexible enough for full Agile deployment while allowing teams that use continuous flow or Kanban to continue with their approach. They can coexist in the same organization. I know this because I have run startups where we used full Agile with Scrum frameworks for product development and used continuous flow via Kanban for all marketing and growth initiatives.

Whether you use a startup-style system like Kanban to manage workflow or a more traditional project management tool, it's absolutely essential to both marketing and innovation success to review your pipeline of initiatives and create a disciplined cadence around prioritization and decision-making. These constraints create focus, velocity, and, most importantly, throughput—a.k.a. the momentum you need for sustainable growth.

In today's world of abundant choice, this applies internally as well; trade-offs are an essential ingredient to success. What you decide not to do is as important as what you decide you will do. You'll need to constantly make adjustments based on the gap between where you are and where you need to be as a team and organization.

Three Areas of Operations

Team organization and performance are as important as the growth initiatives themselves, especially now, with strategy, internal operations, and marketing under more scrutiny than ever before.

The overall productivity, collaboration, decision-making, and performance measurement of teams can be quite complicated, and it becomes even more complicated when you consider how many different types exist—marketing, financial, design, management, and so on. The organizational structure of, for example, marketing teams tends to be decentralized and project based; this can be especially true for companies with distributed global teams. Teams need to make more complicated decisions faster, with an overload of information to sift through.

To evaluate the execution of the strategy, we turn inward to examine the infrastructure and test performance along three key areas: pipeline, people, and process.

Pipeline

Pipeline is all about capturing all potential work and prioritizing what work MUST get done. Are you prioritizing the highest impact initiatives and accessing trade-offs regularly? What is it that you're focused on? Why? What will you stop doing or put in the backlog to prioritize it and apply constraints to your pipeline of potential work?

You can only do what matters most if you actually have a pipeline of everything you could and should be doing to prioritize, and if you make the hard decisions about what moves to the front, what gets backlogged, and what gets killed. For example, if an organization has established a clear pipeline of projects and has determined that only those projects that directly contribute to revenue growth will be prioritized, then any proposed projects that do not meet this criterion will be deprioritized or eliminated. This creates important guardrails that guide decision-making and helps to ensure that limited resources and efforts are focused on the most important tasks and goals to preserve precious runway to achieve the benchmarks (profitability or essential traction) that keep a new venture alive.

Additionally, having guardrails in place can also help to prevent scope creep or distractions from less important or shiny tasks. By establishing clear criteria for prioritization, individuals and teams can stay focused on the tasks that matter most and avoid getting sidetracked by less important activities.

People

Your people—your internal stakeholders—are one of your audiences, and they should be your first customers. How is this culture built? I don't think you *build* culture; you focus on the people and what the brand stands for. Do we have the people we need? Are they in the right seat? Are the people we have in the boat right now who we need for the next stage? Who needs to be developed so they stay? Who's missing? Who can or should go? Identify the missing skills and experience essential to achieve your goals.

People are the most important factor in whether you achieve your goals. Practically and consistently looking at talent gaps and needs is essential to building a sustainable and successful joint marketing and innovation capability. Great talent with diverse voices and perspectives can be the difference between innovation success and failure.

But it's important to be clear about the roles you need to fill and the skill sets you need to acquire. Rather than hiring just for "cultural fit" (which is certainly important), I encourage the innovation leaders I work with to clearly define the roles that need to be filled and the skills that those roles require.

Process

Workflows and resource bandwidth management—or, more often, *mismanagement*—can be the biggest source of bottlenecks. Are you trying to implement new strategies and ventures with old processes and tools? There are multiple tools and solutions to support, automate, or optimize marketing, innovation, and management functions. Using them is not optional anymore, but keeping old workflows, policies, and tools that create significant friction, adoption hurdles, and time lag are also unacceptable. A lean approach to process management is required to speed momentum and time to market to stay competitive. I found that only using the necessary purchase order (PO) and HR systems in corporate innovation created such significant throughput that I was able to minimize the legacy systems I needed to use, even as an executive at Microsoft for Startups.

With this general operating model that takes the best from established brands and validated startups, you will be able to form your business strategy and operations, keeping you on track for forward progress while limiting unnecessary and known risks.

Chapter 7

Pipeline

I prefer the pipeline metaphor over the sales funnel. Funnels narrow your options; pipes keep a steady, even flow. Whether it's water, customers, work, or cash, monitoring this constant flow provides valuable insight into what's working and what's not. Your pipeline is the end-to-end flow of every type of work at your company: what you prioritize; what you focus on in the short, middle, and long term; and the trade-offs you make along the way. This pipeline is my take on how startups can grow and larger corporations can innovate.

For startups, it's all about the hustle—chasing the next customer, closing the next deal, searching for what will add the most value for your customer, and pivoting on the fly. Directing some of the energy you put into the hustle of establishing and directing constant flows (of prospective customers, investors, advisors, partners, and talent) will save you time, energy, and money. It will also help you better understand your market. You need to take the time to build your pipelines carefully, and you need to know when to tap each one.

My perspective on pipeline has changed as the world has become increasingly complex and chaotic. I used to believe that in the post-MVP (minimum viable product) stage of building a company it was important to be ruthlessly focused on a singular vision of the future. This is probably because founders can get so distracted by exploring all the possibilities of their offerings that they run out of runway before getting traction on one possibility or another infusion of capital. This is called *shiny object syndrome*. Founders suffering from it become so focused on chasing the next thing that they don't invest in developing the pipelines that allow them to fully execute their vision.

Instead of focusing exclusively on what you're going to produce (pipeline), you should focus on how you're going to produce it (the process), who's going to produce it (the people), and the various flows that form the inputs for process and people—in other words, pipeline. The startups I currently advise spend 50–70 percent of their focus on crushing their immediate goals, which create value. The remaining time and energy are spent on developing future products, building audiences, creating use cases, and testing possibilities.

This may sound strange to you, especially since I've spent so much time pushing you to have a crystal-clear vision and a laser focus on growth. I'm certainly not telling you *not* to be clear about your goals. What I am telling you is not to be so focused that you shut down new ideas and possibilities because you're trying to do this one specific thing and only this one specific thing, in this specific way.

Many founders model their intended success on the success of another startup, meaning that they attempt to wholesale imitate how another company performed—that never works. I'm not talking about copycat startups, but modeling how Airbnb or Amazon built their company as a model of successful startup strategy or operations. At the risk of sounding woo-woo, your company is operating *now*, while the context and world of that other startup is gone. If you're modeling them now, they're likely at an entirely different stage in their journey. Have no fear; you can and absolutely should learn from the successes and failures of other startups and innovators in your space and the ecosystem at large. You can get where you want to go, but your destination and route may not look the way you thought it would.

The point is that what matters most is a dynamic, not static, target. We didn't live in a predictable world before COVID-19, and we certainly don't live in one now. What matters today might not tomorrow, and that dynamic nature is as true for your company as it is for the market at large and the category you have carved out for yourself.

This means that one of your biggest competitive advantages is your ability to regularly groom your backlog, add new activities, and scrutinize what you should cut because it doesn't add or create enough value for your stakeholders. You can only do what matters most if you keep your pipelines full and flowing by making the hard decisions about what moves to the front, what gets backlogged, and what gets killed.

Large enterprises are based on well-established, stable pipelines. Whether it's how cash flows through the organization, how new employees are recruited, or how sales are generated, a well-organized brand has a clear pipeline to accomplish the task. The problem that they face is that any change in the brand ecosystem—whether it's the marketplace for employees, customers, or sales—can break the flow and cause a catastrophe. The very stability of the pipelines becomes a liability in an uncertain or chaotic environment.

The Types of Flow

Picture this: You're running or swimming a relay, and as you steadily approach the end of your lap and are getting ready to let the next person go, you drop the baton or forget to tap the end of the pool. It's a hiccup that disrupts the entire race for your team, and while you can still continue and maybe even manage to win, you've failed to achieve flow. The concept has often been used in relation to spiritual guidance and reaching a state of mind to perform better in your everyday life, and the same can be applied to businesses.[1] I'm not encouraging the intensive and obsessive dedication to a single task as a state of flow but rather reaching a state of continuous flow where the brand or startup is making progress.

Information Flow

For most companies, information flow is the most critical type of flow but also the hardest to manage. Information is everywhere, and we generate more every day. Figuring out who needs to know what and when can quickly become an overwhelming burden. Traditionally, information in an organization flowed down from the top or up from the bottom (mostly the former). These days, information flows in many different directions—up and down, horizontally across teams or departments, out to in, and even diagonally through different levels or divisions. Dizzying, right?

So how can you successfully manage something that has so many directions at the same time? How can anyone in the organization find out what they need to know? I find that establishing basic information flows is critical to a company's or team's success. There are many, many different approaches to and tools for what is often referred to as *knowledge management*. Much will depend on what kind of organization you're in and what your business goals are. There are a few basic questions that will lay the groundwork for how to approach information flows. These have been formulated by Slack, but the principles are universal:[2]

- Are employees unable to find the assets or information they need to complete their job tasks quickly?
- Are employees unable to quickly refer to past records and reports in order to track progress and trends?
- Are employees unable to provide information to the right people in the right departments?
- Are employees unaware of company-wide policies?

Asking yourself these questions is a good place to start. Good information flow requires time and attention. There are a number of tools that can help you create an information flow system within your company. Find the one that works for you and stick with it.

Talent Flow

Talent flow is when the business smoothly fills not only current positions but potential future ones. Savvy startups focus on how they can hire, grow, and keep good talent. It's different from succession planning; the talent pipeline flows through recruiting new talent to fill new positions, obviously, but also to constantly look for amazing talent to fill gaps in existing skill and experience sets, even if the seats or budget are not yet open. Succession planning is used to build a bench of seasoned talent to fill existing or future leadership or experienced roles within the company, often starting some of these potential future leaders as advisors and board members.[3] Strong brands focus on internal culture and open organizational values.[4] They keep succession planning transparent, with input from all levels of the organization.

Startups strive to emulate successful brands' cultures to become competitive and attractive to new hires. Strong leadership qualities that emulate the startup's culture and values must be clearly communicated and reinforced within the entire organization. As the startup matures, talent becomes critical in its continued financial and operational success.

Mature brands understand the importance of not only hiring the right people but mentoring them to become future leaders within the brand's organization. They incorporate strong mentorship programs and leverage continuous improvement and learning not only in operational efficiency but also in employee skills and capabilities. This, in turn, generates internal brand loyalty and builds the brand's external reputation.[5]

Talent pipelines are not built and executed overnight. Experienced brands spend a large percentage of overhead capital on their talent to ensure cohesion and the right fit. Careful consideration of all costs to attract and retain talent, including training and development, salaries, cost of living allowances, and maintaining a competitive work environment (remote, hybrid, or office space) must be taken into account when hiring new employees. When done right, both employee and employer satisfaction is elevated, and it creates the ideal environment for any venture to thrive.

Idea Flow

Idea flow is everything your team comes up with, large and small, to serve the vision of your company. It's important to create an environment that keeps the ideas for both major and minor improvements flowing. Big brands have trouble here because they are often built on a consensus model, which discourages robust ideation, especially deviation from the norm. The best startups, on the other hand, take an experimental approach by creating smaller, safe-to-fail experiments to test various hypotheses. Both enterprises and startups can make the mistake of not ensuring that there's enough diversity of opinion in the decision-making process.

What's most important is keeping the ideas flowing and not worrying too much about where they come from. That intern who's getting coffee may have an idea for an incremental change that can improve the way that work gets done around your office. Who knows? Keeping a steady flow of ideas is critical, and it's easier to do that if you're not limiting where they come from.

Workflow

One type of flow that deserves attention is workflow. One of the biggest problems I see in every type of organization is too much work in process. And as a serial entrepreneur I can admit, it's easy to create too much flow. Many organizations I work with can't figure out why they're not accomplishing more—look how busy everyone is! It could be argued that busyness is exactly what's keeping you from getting work done.

Workflow is something that needs to be constantly monitored and calibrated with appropriate capacity in the system. Constantly increasing the amount of work in process simply ensures that it will be impossible to successfully execute anything. Too much flow prevents throughput. If you, as a leader, want your team to operate at the highest level, you must communicate that you are more interested in the quality of work and speed of a limited work set than in quantity at a given time. Quantity over time is a positive metric, and with a narrow work in progress (WIP) pipeline of no more than three-to-five things per team member, or sometimes even team, you'll get the appropriate workflow—and throughput—to be shipping work smoothly and on a regular basis. This helps you get to market with ideas faster than your competitors can, which gives you an edge and helps you win!

A lot of companies employ Kanban boards to visualize their workflow, but they often ignore the workflow principles that underlie the Kanban system. David J. Anderson, who was one of the early developers of the method, broke it down into two types of principles and six practices as you can see in Table 7.1.

CHANGE MANAGEMENT PRINCIPLES	SERVICE DELIVERY PRINCIPLES
Start with what you do now	Focus on customer's needs and expectations
Agree to pursue incremental, evolutionary change	Manage the work, not the workers
Encourage acts of leadership at all levels	Regularly review the network of services

Table 7.1. Kanban principles, https://kanbanize.com/kanban-resources/getting-started/what-is-kanban.

I have found that understanding and embracing the method beyond just a visualization of work in process on a board can lead to greater efficiencies than simply introducing an ever-increasing amount of work into the system. For example, while I was writing this book, my team used Trello to organize and track the progress we were making, and we modeled our workflow style to reflect Agile project management. We broke down the large deliverables into bite-size, manageable tasks and often worked in iterations and loops of development, editing, and feedback.

I encourage you to think of these as actual pipes. What can flow where you need things to go? Which ones do you need to turn up right now, and which ones can you turn off for the moment?

Bottlenecks

Each of your pipelines will have bottlenecks or constraints that are beyond your control. It's important to examine all the systems in your organization regularly in order to spot where potential blockages may pop up. It is important to keep all of these pipelines clear. Bottlenecks impede your progress by delaying customer delivery and therefore satisfaction, creating employee friction, losing opportunities, and costing you money. But let's remember that a bottleneck is not the same as a constraint. Constraints are *what we can't have more of* and are there to be managed, not cleared. Managing constraints is how great leaders prioritize and identify opportunities for improvement. Bottlenecks are *what keeps us from moving*. And we all know that stagnation equals death.

Training and development is an example of a bottleneck that cuts both ways. For big brands, it is seen as an activity that could take up to a month to be done. It is interfering with the employees' work and adding confusion as new concepts, systems, and tools are thrown at them to start implementing right away. On the other hand, the lack of training and development prevents startups from having a consistent and steady training flow, which impacts people's performance. It is sometimes overlooked and not invested in.

There's never enough time, money, people, or resources. The question is how those constraints affect your decision-making process. Do you allow them to drive your decision process, or do you use them to your advantage when making decisions? Constraints can be a way to inspire your team to use creative approaches to problem-solving. And maintaining them in that mindset is important for keeping the feeling of lack or scarcity at bay.

Your pipelines and the constraints inherent in each will affect all your decision-making. Obviously there are constraints that will limit your ability to make decisions. The key is to find ways to make the constraints unleash innovation and creativity.

As a CMO and founder, I have experienced blockages and constraints a number of times, often being called in to help a peer with a turnaround when it's already too late. So I would rather tell you how to respond than have to be the plumber you call when you've lost all flow and have a month of runway. There are many root causes to these blockages, but I've most often seen them run from three main faucets. They each might seem positive but can hinder your work and idea flow if they are overcomplicated or incorrectly implemented.

Organizational Structure

Decision-making is a key component of any organization, but too many levels or a complicated structure will result in the decision-making process being slowed almost to a stop. This can ruin the flow of any startup or brand, especially when working with new innovations. Slowed work processes can also lead to increased costs and can decrease the performance of the rest of the company. If no one is willing or able to make the decision from the top, does your staff have the necessary clarity and guardrails to effectively take the lead and uphold the flow?

Incentive Systems

Are you incentivizing the right behavior? I'm not just talking about compensation here but also about how the organization deals with all the thousands of interactions that happen every day, both internally and externally. At big brands, the incentive structure is set by a centralized body that may not have any firsthand knowledge of what's happening at the team level. At many startups, the incentives tend to be ad hoc and not equally distributed throughout the organization. Zappos famously gave their employees full authorization to solve $50 worth of customer problems without management authorization. This empowered the employees to satisfy the customer first, quickly, and with less friction. On the other hand, a startup I worked with kept organizing adventure trips for the staff to build team bonds. That was great for most of the staff, but it was uncomfortable for those not interested in skiing, hiking, rafting, or climbing. These incentives failed to capture the interest of the entire team as it grew, and while it may be nearly impossible to satisfy everyone, take care to craft an incentive system that works to benefit the majority and not disqualify the minority. So while incentives are captured in more than one way, they need to add to the company culture and establish positive interactions at every front.

Process Frameworks

Many organizations try to embrace process frameworks without completely understanding all the implications of that way of work. It's critical to examine not just whether your team is applying the framework but also whether it's actually helping get the work done.

Many large organizations use the Six Sigma method exclusively, which may not be the best approach to leading innovation. However, the framework is baked into all of the team's dependencies and interactions with the company.

Many of the startups and ventures I consult embrace the Agile framework without fully understanding its limitations for different parts of the organization or how to adapt it successfully. My approach to Agile in marketing may not look exactly the same as the Agile practiced by the development team. How leaders approach the implementation of the framework in other departments tells me a lot about how well they understand it.

Flow of Value

The word *value* gets thrown around a lot, even by me, but in my estimation, for startups, value is the ultimate filter for decision-making and trade-

> *Making decisions is what makes you the leader, and what drives those decisions is value.*

offs. Making decisions is what makes you the leader, and what drives those decisions is value. Always ask yourself, *Will this activity or feature meet customer needs?* Then conduct an exercise to validate that value by testing its desirability for the customer, its technical feasibility, and its business viability. This exercise originated from design company IDEO in the 1990s as a way to achieve innovation when building a new business.[6]

Desirability

Achieving customer desirability means having a solution that is alluring, appealing, and satisfying to the customer. Look through a customer-centric lens, or, ideally, let customers do it for you and confirm that their needs are met (no assumptions here!). Start asking yourself what and how they hear about you. What keeps them coming back to your company? Does the market want this right now?

Feasibility

Feasibility is an organization's ability to successfully build for and deliver to the customer's demands. Studies are conducted to ensure the organization can adapt to the changing needs of business. Ensure that your solution can deliver to the specifications that the customer deems desirable. Ideally, this also means the proposed solution is easily or conveniently doable. Some envisioned solutions have not technically ever been executed. Is this new product or feature within the company's capabilities? Can you access a resource; if not, who can? Does it strengthen your current business? What needs to be in place behind the scenes to deliver? Can this solution be delivered at a larger scale?

Viability

Can the solution sustain itself? This starts with the business and financial model but often includes assessing whether the potential liabilities and risks of a solution or its market are reasonable to overcome. Regulation can easily kill the viability of certain solutions and is often market reliant.

Now that we have a clear understanding of what questions to ask in this exercise, let's think about a relatively recent market: how electric vehicles (EVs) approached desirability, feasibility, and viability in their development for the consumer market.

Desirability is a huge factor in the auto industry. Initially, EVs appealed to consumers who were interested in sustainability and reducing fossil fuel emissions. But they also desired all the elements they associated with nonelectric cars—comfort, safety, convenience, affordability, and design. Selling cars has always been about selling luxury and sex appeal, so the manufacturers had to incorporate those features as well as the sustainability message in order to make the vehicles desirable to a broad market.

To make EVs feasible for a mass audience, the research had to focus on the most crucial (but least sexy) part of the machine: the battery. EV battery technology has dramatically improved performance for every application, and it's what made it feasible to manufacture electric vehicles at scale.

The viability of EVs for a mass market depends not just on the manufacturing and distribution of vehicles themselves but also on the development of infrastructure to support them. The vehicles could not become a viable alternative to traditional cars and trucks unless there was a convenient way to charge them. This required the creation of a new infrastructure where charging stations would take the place of traditional gas pumps. Depending on where you are in the world, this infrastructure is still developing. But the availability of ways to charge the vehicle makes them a viable alternative to traditional cars and trucks for everyone.

Now you know that value should be the basis of your pipeline prioritization and decision-making. As you keep your pipeline full and make the hard calls on what moves through to support your momentum and what becomes a trade-off to flow, you must search for and validate what creates value for your customers. Remember the gap? This is that.

And Finally...

Each pipeline needs to be kept flowing properly, so that they can each regulate the others when necessary. Otherwise, when even one of them is only partly blocked, it damages the whole system. For example, information flow profoundly affects idea flow in an organization. Generating ideas that benefit a company's overall vision and strategy is only possible if there is access to the intelligence that resides in the system. There should be no impediments to momentum and circulation.

Imagine your dreams come true and you are suddenly flooded with new customers eager for your product or service, but you don't have enough staff or a pipeline. Now you have to do some fast hiring, increasing your talent flow, which strains cash flow. Meanwhile, there's no time to train them or explain all your processes, so workflow gets bogged down as the team is overwhelmed with work. Since the organization is now in a totally reactive mode, the ability to generate new ideas for products, marketing, or processes grinds to a halt.

I know, this seems like a nice problem to have—and it may be in the short term. But in the long term, this scenario can damage your ability to create a successful future for your organization. If you had a pipeline of talent available for that demand surge and investors or banks, you could quickly get the cash to fill the demand surge. You'd be able to quickly act on the dream scenario every innovator is hoping for. All of this is my way of saying that you should constantly create flow and seek balance.

Kevin at Big Brand

Kevin is on a Zoom call with Meg, Jim, and Samantha. Three on one—not great odds. Their category discovery went well, but things have been slower than expected, and their team hasn't delivered anything concrete yet. But Kevin and his team have been preparing for this meeting all week. Armed with their questions and the insights from the

continued

assumption and persona mapping, Kevin is ready to engage with the MDs.

"Well, when are you going to launch something?" Meg asks. "We've got to show progress as soon as possible."

"What's the impact on the existing product workflow?" Samantha chimes in. "We plan all our product launches months in advance, and I don't even know what you're working on over there."

Kevin takes a deep breath.

"I understand your concerns," he says. "We are trying to deliver to the quarterly schedule, but new things take time. We want to make sure we're delivering value to the customer and profitability to the company. And this means we needed to spend time on figuring out the product–market fit (PMF) and making sure our customers actually want our product before moving forward. We're optimistic, but it is a thoughtful process now so we can speed up once customers are on board. That doesn't happen overnight.

"I have some questions about your expectations and a reasonable timeline for our next product. Do you want incremental changes, or are we going for a moon shot, or both?"

"That's a good question," Jim says. "I haven't projected budgets out past eighteen months. Is that the duration of the project, Meg?"

Meg is clearly not ready to be put on the spot. "I pitched this experiment to see if we could create sustainable innovation at Big Brand. I'm waiting to see what Kevin can deliver in this eighteen-month cycle before we decide whether to continue."

"That's not a great way to foster creativity," Kevin says. Tiff is really rubbing off on him, he realizes. "Short term, we can deliver incremental changes, but it makes it hard to deliver a sustainable innovation effort with long-term profitability when we know the clock is winding down. We're looking at every aspect of customer value that we can deliver. Some of our ideas can have an immediate impact, but we also want to focus on how to keep the innovation pipeline flowing."

"It does hamstring them a bit, Meg," Samantha adds. "I'm curious about the timeline. Do you think the company is ready to commit to a long-term innovation investment? Or should the team be focused on helping me change color palettes?"

Kevin says, "Working with a team from all the different departments at Big Brand has introduced different ways to innovate and determine outcomes that satisfy everyone's needs. This project is becoming about more than what we make and who we're making it for—it's also about how we make it.

"We need to revisit the incentive structure for this project. I can't just keep telling the team that all the extra work they're doing will be reflected in their standard performance review. I would like the three of you to think about what else we're able to do for them inside our existing compensation structure.

"Meg, I understand that you need results—and soon. Jim, I'm aware of project costs. The team will take those things into consideration, as well as answer Samantha's process questions. We want to run a hackathon, open to every department; the team will determine the objective. If it's

continued

successful, we can run them regularly to find products and services that meet customer needs within the existing Big Brand process while fostering new ways of work and gaining buy-in across the organization."

"I thought hackathons were only for startups," Jim says.

"A hackathon is just a way to crowdsource problems or questions with the SMEs who have the talent and know-how to prototype solutions with the context of our customer, resources, and category in mind," Kevin says. "The team will run through how things work, what the time constraints are, and the questions to be answered."

Jamal and Sarah at Struggling Startup

After yet another argument with Sarah about how to structure workflow and product launches, Jamal reached out to his mentor, Alex, and invited him to dinner with Sarah. He's hoping that Alex can coach both of them in developing a more productive way to work.

Jamal immediately starts peppering Alex with questions. Sarah picks up on this energy, and they lay out every problem they're experiencing.

"Whoa," Alex says. "I think we're going to need a bottle of wine and some food before we dive in. Also, I'd like you to identify your biggest problem or roadblock to progress first."

Once they've settled on their orders, Sarah starts. "I think our biggest issue is that we don't have the resources and staff to properly execute our ideas.

"If you wait to have everything you need, you're never going to get anything done. You're stuck on the way you used to do things at your old job, but you're operating in a completely different environment. Nothing will ever be perfect, and it's not going to be easy. You say you've already identified a good PMF. Now you should shift your focus to how to deliver in an efficient, profitable way. At this stage, you should be focused on delivery, efficiency, and fire testing. You truly have PMF and validated costs for acquisition that you can scale. Don't overpromise and underdeliver to customers, but don't strain your resources or your team either."

"But how do we figure out how to do that?" Jamal asks. "We seem to prioritize different things. I'm focused on how we can ship product efficiently, while Sarah is more focused on the team performance and culture."

Sarah reluctantly nods in agreement.

"You're making this an either/or question when it's really both/and," Alex sighs. "You can't ignore either."

"But we don't have the bandwidth for that," Sarah replies. "We're both stretched to the breaking point, our investors are on our backs, and the team is close to mutiny."

"I'm glad you didn't wait until things were bad to contact me!" Alex exclaims. "You two have fallen into a classic trap. You keep focusing on one aspect of the work at a time instead of thinking about flow. When you're thinking about what you're going to build, you have to consider how you're going to build it, and within your resource constraints, *at the same time.*"

continued

"He's right!" Sarah says. "I think we've created artificial boundaries in our thinking and planning that inhibit the workflow. We need to take a more holistic approach up front."

"But we can't start over!" Jamal exclaims.

"The good news is you don't have to," Alex says. "You've already determined the customer need you want to fill, but you can't actually build the product you're proposing because of resource constraints, right?"

Jamal and Sarah nod.

"So you need to reexamine the product's scope—not a fundamental change, more of an edit. What can you build that will allow you to launch a profitable product that customers want with the available workflow infrastructure? You're not starting from scratch; you're just adjusting to the constraints."

"So what's our next step?" Jamal asks.

"What do you think it is?" Alex replies. "I can't do this for you; no one can. Only you can answer that question. You need to learn from what's not working in order to build something that will. Struggling isn't fun, but it's the only way to move forward. Start with how you might break it into smaller releases."

"Okay, great. You've given us a lot to think about," Sarah says. "I can see ways that we can think about workflow differently."

"And I can see how we can start to think about product in terms of workflow and shifting the workload to something that feels more doable," Jamal adds.

"Great. Let's get a dessert menu," Alex says.

Chapter 8

People

Your people are the most important factor in marketing, growth, and organizational success. Great talent brings meaning to formal workflows and makes smart use of the technology to support the process and maximize output. But while that's all true, it can be difficult to know how to find and cultivate the right people, much less how to turn those individuals into a DREAM team.

When I'm called in to "fix" a company, I always start with a people assessment to help calibrate the current state of the organization. I focus on the dynamic between the individual and the team and on the crucial soft skills that put that individual over the top.

I will start by telling you the story of a thousand failures. I won't disclose the name of the company (for obvious reasons), so let's call it Badeas—for bad ideas. The problems started when the company did. The founder of Badeas had no strong desire to solve a problem or enhance his customers' experiences. He just wanted to start a company to "make it"—to get rich, get out of corporate, and call himself a founder. Without any strategic direction for the company, and no real growth strategy, and despite focusing on "hustling for sales," $10 million in revenue, and a decent B2B pipeline, there was still no product–market fit.

This is how far you can go down the wrong path without something necessary for success. Without product–market fit or any pattern recognition to get there, startups get caught up in this "hustle to grow" hype that has no stability in sight and ends up burning out your team—and your company—in the process.

Badeas acquired a smaller startup, which had one technical cofounder and one nontechnical cofounder. Badeas's founder named the nontechnical cofounder head of marketing, even though that particular person had no deep marketing, sales, or brand expertise and had never scaled a company before. Translation: The founder took a talented person and put them in a role that did not align with their skill set, experience, or passion just to put them somewhere. It was the blind leading the blind as far as defining success went.

I should point out here that the nontechnical cofounder was a high performer with grit and quick-thinking skills. He also genuinely wanted the team and company to succeed. However, even a smart, committed person cannot be expected to know how to define success for their reports and lead their team to victory without some advice or help from people who have won at the game they're playing now, have subject matter expertise in those fields, and can help define success. If the Badeas founder had arranged for the nontechnical founder to have some advisors or mentors with deep startup sales and marketing experience, things would have gone differently and *faster*. One of the many lessons to learn from Badeas is the importance of your leadership values and company culture in building a successful team.

Culture and Values

The Badeas founder mismanaged the talents of a high-level employee, which is just one example of the number of times that type of mistake occurred at the company. On the surface, this looks like a hiring and management problem, but it's more than that; it's inextricably connected to a failure to establish and adhere to a culture and values from the jump. If the Badeas founder had created and enforced guidelines about how the company operated and what should be important to each team member, they would have saved themselves a lot of heartache—and money and time. Remember: Runway is precious fuel.

Culture Fit

I don't think that leaders necessarily understand what it means to hire someone who is a "culture fit" for their company. A lot of hiring managers translate it as the candidate getting along with others in the break room or at a Friday happy hour. That is ideal, of course, because you do want to hire people who will get along with each other. However, "culture fit" goes beyond just that; leaders have to vet people who not only fit in with the rest of the company but also fit into the established business culture and their own leadership style. You know how important your culture and values are! They create energy, clarity, momentum, guardrails, and buy-in. A lack of strong culture and lived values leads to dissonance, which can range from a general feeling of uneasiness that things at your company "just aren't right," to utter catastrophe.

Any and all gaps between stated and lived values are immediate and persistent liabilities for young ventures and, as we've seen many times in the news, established brands. One of my favorite startup examples of how a focus on the right kind of culture fit can pay big dividends is CB Insights.[1] The founders chose to build a culture of learning and knowledge. They recruit people who are hungry for both formal learning opportunities, as well as learning by doing. They don't just talk the talk, however. They support their employees' journey with educational stipends and an environment that encourages them to explore all the different roles in the organization. This commitment to being a learning organization has allowed them to seamlessly scale from 10 employees to 180.[2]

If you've ever worked in a corporate environment, you may have heard that values are meant to be aspirational, not lived. Nope. There should be no gap between a company's stated values and the employee experience. Aspirational values are essentially meaningless. Lived values are part of the company's DNA. This doesn't mean companies will always execute them perfectly every day; I understand that you're human, and so is everyone on your team. But even if you can't always *execute*, you can always *embody* your values and own your behavior when you don't deliver.

> *A gap—or, God forbid, a gulf—between your values and reality is a huge distraction to your entire team; it sucks up energy, breaks focus, and sows mistrust.*

A gap—or, God forbid, a gulf—between your values and reality is a huge distraction to your entire team; it sucks up energy, breaks focus, and sows mistrust. That combination of bad energy can spread like wildfire in a young organization, where teams are tight and transparency is high. Even in larger organizations, those gaps can crush growth and customer trust. Articulate and live your values, and your people strategy will be a lot easier to formulate and execute.

Well-Being

While living your values is important, what you really want to establish with your business culture is a sense of well-being. "Well-being comes from one place, and one place only—a positive culture." I'm not quoting myself here (though I do say things like this on real and virtual stages); I'm quoting Emma Seppälä, author of *The Happiness Track* and codirector of wellness for the Yale Center for Emotional Intelligence.[3] Creating a happy, healthy, and positive culture is something I've always deeply believed in. A positive culture is an absolutely essential ingredient for success.

Seppälä's research supports what I found in my twenty years of experience as a leader in chaotic environments, that a positive workplace culture boils down to six essential characteristics:[4]

- Caring for, being interested in, and maintaining responsibility for colleagues as you would for a friend
- Providing support for one another, including offering kindness and compassion when others are struggling
- Avoiding blame and forgiving mistakes, a.k.a. assuming best intent
- Inspiring one another at work
- Emphasizing the meaningfulness of the work
- Treating one another with respect, gratitude, trust, and integrity

When these six characteristics are present in your culture, your team will thrive. Creating this type of environment reaps all kinds of rewards—loyalty, engagement, productivity, innovation, and success.

So how can leaders cultivate a positive culture and workplace well-being? When it comes to workplace culture, I begin by saying that I apply all the same rules to myself as to my team. In other words, I lead by example. If I tell the team that I don't expect hundred-hour work weeks, I make a point of not spending all my time at the office, and I maintain a regular schedule.

I try to practice empathy and compassion. This isn't about sympathy. This is about recognizing that everyone's life (and work) experience is different and also ever-changing. Giving people the space to adapt their work life to the circumstances of their real life is key to growth and retention.

Consistency is also key—not only consistency in the type of organizational culture but also in the expectations of how this culture will operate. Too often I see the cultural norms ignored when it comes to a high-performing individual in an organization. On my teams, if there is a zero-tolerance policy about gender inclusivity, for example, individuals who violate it are dismissed regardless of how "productive" they are.

I also aim to make respect the basis of all my interactions, both personal and professional. At work, that means I try to treat everyone with the same level of professionalism, regardless of their role in the organization. Some of my most valuable team members started out as interns. They stayed not because of the opportunities (okay, a little because of the opportunities) but because we collectively made an effort to make them feel like a valued member of the team.

This isn't all there is to it, obviously, but these four precepts are a good place to start.

The Sixth Man

Startups focus on hiring rock stars, ninjas, gurus, and other words that are just woefully misused in this context. I call these people *players*. You certainly want your first key hires to be excellent players—your starters, if you will, even though you have no bench to back them up. But you also want to hire each of them as part of a cohesive team, so it's important to always keep the shape of your entire team in mind as you hire. This doesn't mean you shouldn't look for amazing people; it means you need to look for the *right* amazing people who will work well together.

A great sports analogy of this is Red Auerbach's theory of the sixth man.[5] In professional basketball, the sixth man is not a starting player but is the first and most often called up from the bench to play. Many famous sixth men spend as much time on the court as starters do, and having a strong sixth man is a powerful indicator of team excellence. Extremely talented NBA players have been the sixth man—Kevin McHale of the Boston Celtics and Toni Kukoč of the Chicago Bulls, for example. Those teams are best known for Larry Bird and Michael Jordan, but they would not have won all those championships without their sixth man.

Basketball coaches have outlined the important qualities a great sixth man should have. First is knowing their team's systems as well as the starting players do.[6] Second, they must be a positive force on the floor. Third, the sixth man must be an impact player who changes the game when they step onto the court. Fourth, they focus on fitness and endurance. Fifth, they have the ability to play both offense and defense. Scoring ability plus being a strong defensive asset is key. Sixth is hunger. The sixth man should always be trying to break into the starting lineup, the elite level of the leadership team.

You may not value physical condition or defensive skills as much as the Boston Celtics do, but most of those skills work just as well on your company's team. You need those skills on your team and to have players beyond the superstars.

Building a DREAM Team

An individual's skills must work well within a group because that is how we now work; a *Harvard Business Review* study found that managers and employees spend upward of 50 percent more time in collaborative activities than they did two decades ago and that at many companies more than 75 percent of an employee's day is spent communicating with colleagues.[7]

Your team is your first customer and one of your most important stakeholders. I'm not going to go into detail about the hard skills you should look for in specific hires, as that will depend on what and how you're building your company, but I do want to take time here to talk about what it really means to build a DREAM team because it is the only way to create breakthrough success!

I've always told my past venture and startup clients that to build a DREAM team you need to evaluate each candidate on their soft skills with as much detail as their technical skills. People can learn techniques, but there are many soft skills that cannot be trained. People can get more experience, acquire subject matter expertise, or learn technical skills, but it's almost impossible to teach someone how to learn, adapt, analyze, make difficult decisions, be a team player, lead by example, and raise the entire team up.

Figuring out whether people have those soft skills is a skill unto itself, which is why I'm a big fan of behavior-based interviewing. Behavior-based interviewing "points to past performance as the best predictor of future performance," says Paul Glatzhofer, VP of Talent Solutions.[8] In short, instead of asking hypothetical questions about how a candidate *would* behave in a specific situation, I ask how the candidate *did* behave in a situation. I ask follow-up questions and get details so that I'm getting the real story and not an anecdote that the candidate has prepared in advance. Their answers give me real insight into whether they have the soft skills I require. I also like to ask about their habits and behaviors.

When assessing a current team's performance, preparing to grow a thriving team, or starting from scratch, I use a simple framework for top-of-mind awareness about the values I want my team to reflect. When I say *simple*, I don't mean *easy*; this framework is hard-won from years of experience with literally hundreds of different team members. Its creation also required me to do a great deal of work on myself as an individual contributor and as a leader. This means that you can now benefit from my successes, reboots, missteps, and outright failures without having to experience them all yourself. You're welcome!

Entrepreneur and journalist Shane Snow has written extensively on team building, including a wonderful book, *Dream Teams: Working Together Without Falling Apart.*[9] I have always advised startups to build a DREAM team as well, although my approach is a little different from Shane's (great minds work alike, no?). My approach to building a DREAM team starts with a simple question: What would this look like if it were easy? Then I incorporate the following guidelines into the answer to that question to build out what the ideal team would look like:

Lauren's DREAM guide

- Diversity
- Responsibilities
- Environment
- Agency
- Motivation

Diversity

Diversity is not just about capital-D diversity from an HR sense (having people on your company website who look different from each other), and it's not checking the boxes on hiring criteria that are mostly focused on ethnicity. I'm talking about diversity at every level—educational, socioeconomic, geographic, and level of experience. This is the same diversity that allows innovation to thrive and bring fresh and varied ideas to the table.

For example, many of my past venture and startup clients have told me they conduct "targeted" searches when recruiting. Unfortunately, this often means they rely on a few well-defined sources, like certain universities (including their alma mater), or searching LinkedIn for people who have worked for Big Company A with specific qualifications. If you're doing that, you need to stop right now. There are so many talented women, BIPOC, and other underrepresented candidates out there, and it's on you as a leader to examine your own assumptions and biases about the candidates you recruit and interview or where you find talent and how that might be creating bias by limiting the diversity in the talent pool. I doubt any founders set out to hire only white men, but only hiring from expensive schools generally means by default hiring people with a lot of privilege. Privilege does not equal talent. And it certainly reduces diversity.

The startup world prides itself on innovation, disruption, and thinking outside of the box, and yet, time and time again, I see founders limiting their searches (and offers) to Ivy League grads. It blows my mind. I can tell you that limiting your search to who you know will certainly bring in a lot of smart people who *all have a similar perspective.*

Responsibilities

I look for individuals who not only meet the qualifications for the current role but are also adaptable enough to grow with changing and expanding roles. For example, I hired someone in early February 2020, shortly before the global pandemic shut down the

United States. Her original role was to manage network-building, thought-leadership strategies, and personal business and events alongside my role at Microsoft for Startups, which, of course, was rendered obsolete by the shutdown; there were no events to manage.

During her interview, I stressed that I was looking for someone with a specific core set of skills (which she had) but who was also comfortable dealing with uncertainty and ambiguity (which she was enthusiastic about doing) and was willing to learn from others. Needless to say, those qualities were tested almost immediately after she started work. On her first official day, our team was in the throes of decision-making about whether or not we could still greenlight the annual SaaStr conference, an event we had been preparing for in sixty-plus-hour weeks for two months. Almost nothing about her first month went the way we thought it would, but she met all of those challenges head-on and succeeded with flying colors. She adapted her new role and its numerous, ever-changing responsibilities like a champ and has proven herself over and over again to be a valuable team member in many ways.

It doesn't matter what you're hiring someone to do or whether your newest hire will face an unprecedented national lockdown. What matters is that your company will grow, pivot, and change, and you need to make sure that everyone you bring on—especially in the first year—is ready and able to tackle all of that with you.

Environment

I aim to build learning-focused environments for all of my teams. This involves drawing clear lines of accountability and responsibility; within those guardrails, however, I build safe-to-fail experiments, which allow the team to learn and implement our findings quickly.

I also create psychologically safe environments by focusing on trust and transparency. This takes calibration, both from me and from members of my team—especially the newer members who haven't been fortunate to have this kind of work environment in the past. My admin at Microsoft for Startups was shocked when she originally joined the team as a legacy Microsofter. She was surprised this ethos was embodied by my team and wasn't just something I had said and set expectations for during the recruitment process. After accepting that this was lived and not just a stated way of work, she started to fully embody open and transparent communication. In the end, she not only trusted in the joint problem-solving process but championed it.

I am constantly assessing whether a certain level of transparency will overwhelm my team or keep them in the dark on important topics for too long. It also requires clarity on preferred communication channels, cadence, timing, and styles. Setting a communication cadence is especially important when your team works in multiple time zones or on offset schedules. This book, for example, was produced by a team that was located across Spain, Peru, El Salvador, Miami, Austin, and NYC. As the team leader, I had to find a communication cadence that made sure my entire team received actionable information in a timeframe that both worked for them and contributed to the success of the project.

Every aspect of communication and collaboration needs to be considered. These are important boundaries to set not only for my team but also for myself, particularly with regard to my own health and performance. I would never expect someone on my team to answer emails or log onto a call at 11:00 p.m. their time, and they know it. The current global 24/7 work-from-home situation can lead to burnout very quickly on all sides.

I've always found that the more transparent I am with my team, the more they trust me. Trust is something we all talk up as a cornerstone of our businesses and leadership styles, but most leaders do not actually practice the simple behaviors that create an environment of trust, even as they come up with strategies to achieve what trust brings: collaboration, cooperation, inclusivity, and productivity. Those cannot truly exist without trust.

I want to point out that openness and trust do not mean that anything goes. For example, my team is well aware that I will not tolerate disrespect, and if it presents itself, I get to the bottom of things immediately and repair the damage that has been done. Seeing me hold myself to the standards I set for my team does more for them than any speech I might make.

Agency

If you hire well, you should be giving your people both ownership of their work and the freedom to do it; agency is having control over their environment. In a world where we feel increasingly unstable, it is empowering to have a bit of control. So harness it!

When possible, I ensure that, apart from necessary meetings and communications, all team members can set their own work hours. The goal here is not working for the sake of the clock but rather about contribution, impact, and outcomes. My people own how they get their work done, when and, these days, where as well.

I also leave space for discovery and development for all of my staff. I am, of course, responsible for them financially, as every business owner is, but I like to also support them emotionally and make sure that I provide learning opportunities for everyone on my staff. I encourage them to explore what they're really interested in, both on and off the job. My consulting practice exposed my team to several different industries, and I encouraged them to explore each. As a result, several of them now work in finance, health tech, fitness, retail, and beauty verticals. They discovered a passion for these industries while on consulting gigs, and I encouraged them to develop those passions into a career path.

Motivation

Motivation is all on you as a leader. Productivity comes from individual team members, but the energy, momentum, and urgency that drive momentum come from the leader. Momentum is contagious, and you want that focus and drive for impact to spread! How you motivate your team depends on the type of person you are and what you're trying to achieve. I have found that, no matter what your leadership style, imposing a ton of rules and trying to force individual behaviors doesn't work.

So how do I do it? My personal style is very high energy, which my team finds enthusiastic and motivational (hey, I was a group exercise instructor for ten years!). Not everyone finds me motivational though; one particularly talented strategist refers to me derisively as "the Energizer bunny." That being said, even he agrees I provide an outlet for his creativity on every project. Guarantee that everyone on your team is creative in some way and has creative energy to offer when solving any problem or working on any project. You must encourage their agency while creating the environment in which their diversity of opinion, education, background, and experience—regardless of their responsibilities—can be brought to bear.

Motivating your team is not about getting them to work more or better or even smarter. It's about creating opportunities for them to show you what they've got. I believe that attitude is everything. I recognize that my role is to nurture the right attitude, not impose mine on them. And that's how I motivate my team.

Shane Snow has also been thinking and sharing content about how to build a great team. His five-step plan to build a DREAM team dovetails nicely with my own:

- Hire counterintuitively.

- Create an inclusive culture.

- Unite people around a shared purpose.

- Give your team time to think about and work on ideas not directly related to their day-to-day work.

- Accept that they won't be perfect all of the time and focus your leadership energy on strengthening teamwork skills.

These principles should guide you toward making the right decisions for your people and building a productive, engaged team.

Setting and Managing Expectations

Misunderstood and mismanaged expectations are among the leading causes of employee unhappiness, and no one wants unhappy— and, therefore, unproductive—employees. Your managers must be trained to clearly define the goals and objectives they set for their direct reports. One of the ways you do this is by clearly defining the goals and objectives *you* set for them.

You're likely using remote communication more often or with teams that didn't rely on it before. This can muddy the clarity of your message or confuse your teams about their cadence. Be sure to state every delivery request clearly and repeatedly to minimize information loss. A clear delivery request defines what "done" looks like, what "successful" looks like, and what the quantitative and qualitative measurement objectives are.

Engagement

Employee engagement problems always stem from poor management, a toxic culture, or hiring the wrong people to work within a company's existing culture. If you find yourself with an engagement problem, I strongly recommend getting a coach to help you think through how you engage your team, as it is something that is difficult to analyze without an outside perspective. Don't be afraid to sit down with the people who aren't leaning in and have an honest, open heart-to-heart with them about what their blocks are. Founders are usually so invested in their companies that they can take a lack of engagement personally, so consider using a facilitator for this type of meeting (again, outside perspectives can help). If you do all of those things and still have an issue, call me for a fix!

Engagement is closely tied to culture. A strong sense of fulfillment and purpose on the individual level and a strong, trusting relationship with one's manager and peers are the recipe for high levels of employee engagement.

Retention

"People leave managers, not companies."[10] Hoo boy, is this true. How many times has someone you know told you that they're going to quit? How many times has their chief (if not sole) complaint been with their manager? That Venn diagram is as close to a single circle as I've seen.

That retention quote is from Marcus Buckingham's book *First, Break All the Rules: What the World's Greatest Managers Do Differently*. It will amuse you (and not surprise you) to learn that I read that book in high school just for fun. It wasn't assigned for any class; I was just attracted to management because as an athlete I always thought there could be a different, better way to manage people more like coaches did so that they felt supported, thrived, and actually really loved what they did. Even when their manager has to give them hard news or when the last assignment they got wasn't that fun or interesting, those employees still love working with their manager and respect them. I still believe this!

And Finally...

Regardless of what you hear and read, people are still the most important part of your organization. Yes, technology is allowing organizations to automate more and more mundane tasks to increase productivity. But that should be used to free up your people from the lowest-value work to explore creative ways to grow your business. Employee retention and acquisition, engagement, and training will be critical in the future as we all look for ways to reskill the people who understand our business to effectively use the technological innovations that are unfolding faster and faster. We all know it is impossible to remove people entirely from the equation, but as automation allows you to do more with smaller teams, those people will be even more critical to your success. AI will make the human part of what we all do even more important and valuable. Treat your people well; they will always be your most important asset.

Kevin at Big Brand

Every time Kevin thinks he's made progress, some new issue appears. It's like playing Whac-A-Mole. To get some advice, he's meeting with his old business professor, Seth.

"This whole leading-a-new-team thing is trickier than I thought," Kevin says. "The whole team seems unhappy, disconnected, and unmotivated. Half the time they just stare at me, and the other half they complain."

"What are they complaining about?" Seth asks.

"Me, each other, the project, me, the schedule, their compensation structures, me—you get the picture."

"I feel like you need to spend some time getting the team to open up about what's really bothering them," Seth says. "I'd be willing to bet that some of it is a reaction to the uncertainty that any new endeavor generates. And they're not used to this kind of uncertainty at a big corporation."

"Uncertainty!" Kevin nearly spits his coffee. "I've worked to get them recognized performance metrics, outlined clear goals and outcomes, the whole nine yards."

"Yes, but all of this is still new for them," Seth replies. "You need to really dig into the source of their anxiety. Some of it will be individual, but a lot of it will be collective. If they spend most of their time wondering if they're doing the right thing, they'll do a lot less, getting caught in the thought–feeling loop and not executing. Do you remember that technique we covered in class, the five whys?"

"Yes, but isn't that too simple for this situation? Repeatedly asking why seems a bit basic."

"It's a little more than that. The five whys was developed by Sakichi Toyoda in the early days of the Toyota Motor Company. Tachii Ohno further developed it for the Toyota Production System. You don't just randomly start asking why. The point is to ask why five times during the discussion of a problem. Toyoda and Ohno believed that by the fifth why the root cause of the problem will be revealed. The point isn't to make them talk, it's to create a structure and environment that encourages them to share relevant insights and feelings."

"Yeah, I remember, but whenever I try one of these techniques the team resists. They say I'm wasting time or that they already know this stuff. It's frustrating."

"Look, Kevin. Stop feeling sorry for yourself. This is an amazing opportunity for you, but you have to recognize where and when you need help, not just in figuring out what to do and how to do it, but also when to step back and let the team lead, assisted by experts."

"What do you mean? I'm supposed to be leading this team. Won't it be admitting that I failed if I accept that they don't trust me?" Kevin is startled by the direction the conversation has taken.

"No one is asking you to give up or stop leading the team. Leading with vulnerability and authenticity builds a more trusting environment and shows that it's okay to ask for help. Bringing in outside facilitators to allow you to be an equal participant can open up dialogue in a way that having the boss lead the meeting cannot. I'd be delighted to work up a series of exercises with you. Some of my grad students could facilitate the workshop."

continued

Two weeks later, Kevin spends a half-day with Seth working on the exercises and is able to schedule the full-day workshop for the following week. At first, his team is suspicious, but Seth and his students know how to facilitate a group experience so that the team actually enjoys talking about what is bothering them.

That meeting has given Kevin another new angle on leadership. Effective leadership isn't just about what we expect employees to do, it's about providing them with the safety, environment, and tools that they need to make the work happen. He owes Seth and his team, big time.

Jamal and Sarah at Struggling Startup

Jamal and Sarah have regular get-togethers to build team camaraderie, as well as daily standups. But the amount of work and demanding environment mean that team spirit is not enough.

"It's so hard to get this group to work together," Sarah complains. "I keep watching all these videos on building a collaborative environment, team dynamics, blah, blah, blah. I need a break. I'm heading out to that startup meetup. Want to come?"

The speaker at the meetup, Camilla, is a serial entrepreneur. She speaks for over an hour about building effective teams in all her organizations. After the talk, Sarah and Jamal approach her.

"Camilla at the meetup, your talk perfectly diagnosed the

issues we're having in our company," Jamal begins. "If you have some time, we'd love to outline our issues."

"We're struggling to get both teams working together," Sarah adds.

"I'm always happy to talk to people about this journey," Camilla replies. "Let's set up a meeting."

A week later, they are in their conference room with Camilla, the product owner, Nik, and their main investor, Lucas.

"We would have come to you, Camilla," Sarah says.

"It's easier to talk about specific problems in context," Camilla says. "And I'm writing a book about building effective teams, so I'm always on the lookout for extra validation."

"Well, we've got a load of problems for you to have a look at," Jamal grimaces.

"Well, right off the bat, I'd say you have to readjust your attitude to being hopeful about your situation and not jump straight to diagnosing." Camilla says. "Difficulties building a team are part of the founder experience and, frankly, the human experience. The more risk or more intimate, the more you're gonna feel it, and that's not a bad thing."

"I know," Sarah says, "but we can't seem to solve anything."

"Maybe just take a step back and define the problem instead of looking for solutions," Camilla replies. "Talk me through it."

Sarah and Jamal detail the history of their company, with interjections from Lucas and Nik. Twenty minutes later, Camilla holds up her hand.

continued

"Okay," she says. "Let's talk about what you expect the team to accomplish." She begins by asking them to describe their recruiting process.

Jamal takes her through how they recruit, starting with the job descriptions.

Camilla stops him there. "Why do you focus on skill sets and credentials so much?"

"Because we need those abilities to fill a hole on the team," Sarah says.

"But why is it only about skill?" Camilla continues.

"Because without the skills they can't accomplish the task," Jamal replies.

"Why do you think completing a task will move the team toward the desired outcome?"

"Wait!" Nik practically jumps out of his chair. "You're five-whying them?"

Camilla smiles. "If you know about it, why haven't you done it already?"

"I didn't think they would appreciate me asking those kinds of questions," Nik replies.

"There you go," Camilla says, turning to Jamal and Sarah. "You have a team member who knows how to diagnose some of your ills but didn't feel comfortable questioning you. I'm sure Nik and the rest of the team know lots of other ways to map problems.

"You're hiring to a job description rather than looking for individuals who can help you achieve your desired outcome and deliver within your culture. Should they have skill? Yes, but in small teams, it's important to find people who can collaborate on a common goal and also provide extra value that will ultimately help accomplish better business results."

Sarah and Jamal feel a little stunned, but Nik is grinning ear to ear.

"You just perfectly stated what I've been feeling for months, Camilla," Nik says.

"Thanks for recognizing that we have more to offer than just the skill set they thought they were hiring," Nik adds. "They keep telling us about goals, but they aren't as clear on how we can contribute to achieving them."

Chapter 9

Process

P rocess is hard to talk about, mostly because it isn't sexy and is often thought of as a necessary evil. I'm here to tell you, both are indeed true! Process is the unsexy, necessary evil you need when you want to scale and achieve sustainable growth. And the more profitable and predictable you want your growth outcomes, the more necessary it is. So you can ignore it, you can vilify it, but the one thing you cannot do is ignore it, unless you want to most certainly go broke. Let's improve your odds, shall we?

Startups often think they don't need process because hustle and sweat got them where they are. The pre-product–market fit can also be a path to validation, but hustle is not scalable. New ventures in the corporate or hybrid corporation–startup world often can't agree on how much process to build. Most entrepreneurial types simply don't love this work. How's that for honesty? But we have to do it.

Process creation should be approached with an iterative and experimental mindset. Simply copying what works for another company will never succeed in yours. Context is everything when you're talking about a process. It is the lifeline of most corporations, the driving force for impact and value-creation. We want your process to be the ideal balance between a stable structure—for your people's sanity—and an agile approach to innovation to achieve your company's desired outcomes.

One of the things that makes it hard to talk about process is the fact that companies have multiple processes dedicated to solving different problems. Do people work for you? We have an HR process for that. Do you create physical products? There's a manufacturing process. Software or service products? Well, the software development process is a whole industry. And the list goes on. But what all those different things have in common is that they should deliver value to the customer and the organization. If you deliver on or over your promise, people can and very often will stomach all kinds of related growing pains. That's why an experimental approach to designing any process is critical.

Where does process come from?

One of the first big experiments you'll be doing as a founder is choosing your process. You won't know if it works until it either produces good results or fails and instead needs to be iterated, a process of continuous improvement. And nailing a process is necessary for growth—you can give up on expanding your operations if your basic processes aren't working as they should.

Get the processes out of your head and into action. All ideas, whether they succeed or fail, start at an inception stage. However, the process it ends up following is up to its owner; some may just need a quick visual to get the ball rolling, whereas others map out what the entire project could end up looking like.

Next, get clear on how you want to spend your time in your

business or projects. This clarity will allow you to identify the outcome and operations you need to build a process. Then you move on to analyzing which processes you have in place and which ones impact your profit or potential for growth. You will hopefully now know your process and then start taking the opportunity to improve it.

For example, Kayak, the travel search platform, examined their internal processes and realized the contract-signing process was taking up disproportionate time and resources. By experimenting with the new DocuSign e-signature platform (not so new anymore), they could significantly streamline the contract signing process. The digital approach led to improvements in "efficiency, compliance, measuring, and tracking."[1] This is a great illustration of a relatively simple change in process that delivered the desired outcome and had a major impact.

How to Optimize Your Process

When I build a process for people and their ventures, I always begin with the vision, the outcomes, and the performance benchmarks that already exist. It is crucial to take our current state into consideration and know what steps we need to take to perfect the processes in place. This is by no means a linear event, and you'll likely be iterating between what you currently have and the changing standard of the dream and vision.

An effective process cannot emerge without consideration for people and performance; they are the foundation for all effective processes. After all, a process is just a framework that ensures things run smoothly and on the right track. I begin by ensuring that the vision is clear and consistent with the desired outcomes and that benchmarks are aligned with those outcomes. Only then can you build or optimize a process that will get the growth where you want it to be.

How your company is doing what it does is different from how any other company is doing it. That's part of the value proposition you used to get your investors, customers, and other stakeholders on board. So it stands to reason that you need to carefully consider your what and how (and even your when) as you think through how to adapt existing processes. To put it another way, instead of just adopting a certain process because you read that Netflix uses it, research and map out how those processes would play out in *your* company, with your customers, your value prop, and your product. Your company is not Netflix.

But you should learn from Netflix's example. The company makes changes to their process in response to newly identified problems. A recent case in point was their attempt to crack down on password sharing. They have yet to solve it, and instead have taken an experimental approach by tweaking the account process in different countries to see what works best.[2]

Stability and Agility

Whether you're building from scratch or adapting to an existing infrastructure, creating your process requires flexibility, adaptability, and an ability to keep the big picture in mind while focusing on the details—as well as nerves of steel. I am once again emphasizing the balancing act of creating stability while maintaining agility because seriously—it's crucial. Processes are truly where you strike both the balance and the tension between the two for your people, your customers, and growth. Too much process, and the weight will slow you down. Not enough process, and as your team and venture mature, the agility could turn into chaotic instability, which impedes the repeatable processes necessary to scale. Your processes must be steeped in the reality of how your people actually work and how your customers actually use your products and services, not in how you *want* them to.

When I've got my founder hat on, sometimes I have to remind myself that it's so much more effective to leverage my stakeholders' words and behaviors instead of my own expectations. My approach to process is always customer-centric. How can we deliver the most value to our customers (and potential customers) in an efficient, repeatable manner? In too many companies, *customer centricity* is just something you say. But it's not about talking the talk, it's about walking the walk and making the customer's needs the focus of every process and outcome. It's also crucial that your process helps your company meet its objectives and goals, which should also be customer-driven.

Unfortunately, there is no one-size-fits-all way to put your customer at the center of your business processes. There are many frameworks, methods, and tools; some work and some don't. I particularly like the customer centricity model (Figure 9.1) from Stephan MacDonald at the SuperOffice blog.[3]

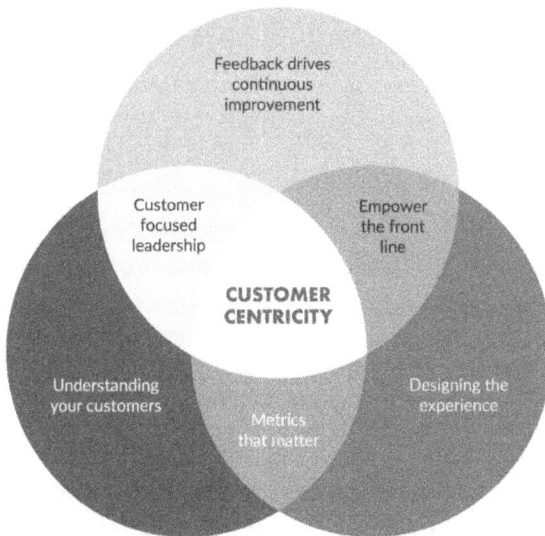

Figure 9.1. Customer centricity.

In this model, every system and process in the organization needs to focus on how the system serves the customer. I love this visualization—it encapsulates a lot of the problems that ventures, large and small, have had with customer centricity. Most organizations overinvest in one of the circles, ignoring the balance you need to be truly customer-centric. Several years ago, I was coaching a startup that was scaling rapidly. The founder was explaining how the company's commitment to customer service was absolute. But when I asked them to walk me through the process, it became apparent that their investment was focused on "designing the experience." While the original core group of employees understood how customer centricity was defined and its importance to the organization, there was no process in place to train new employees in these principles. Nor was there a clearly defined internal feedback system. Over the course of a few months, I worked with the founder and their team to put together customer centricity onboarding resources. Stipends for continuing education in various aspects of customer service were made available to every employee. We also refined existing feedback processes and created some new ones in order to ensure that feedback flowed through the organization. By the end of my engagement, the scale-up venture was set up for customer-centric success.

This is easier said than done, but unless you align your team to a customer-centric system, you cannot build lasting, sustainable success. And that focus starts with *you*. You, the leader, have to focus your decision-making and feedback on creating value for and with the customer.

That focus on customer centricity makes it easier to achieve the balance between stability and agility that I've been talking about. At too many companies, it is mostly hype—a rebranding of traditional marketing, sales, and customer service that involves no fundamental change and delivers little benefit. Genuine customer centricity requires transforming all enterprise functions that affect customers, breaking down the silos between those functions, and building a culture that rewards behaviors aligned with customer success. And what better way to make this happen than to do so in the startup ideation and discovery phase before there are things like high payroll costs eating at your runway and investor expectations to also deliver on?

Cadence and Meeting Structures

You want to run things in a way that sets your team up for success. One way is to structure your meetings for impact. Have you ever seen the meme that reads, "This meeting could have been an email?" Well, that's exactly what we want to avoid. I hate unnecessary meetings, too!

For example, one of my last startup advisory gigs before I took the MD at Microsoft for Startups portfolio role was for a company that was so meeting-heavy that they had trouble actually executing anything. My team and I were initially hired to "fix" (evaluate and streamline) marketing and to build a sustainable growth engine to unlock exponential scale that had stagnated. But as we analyzed the meeting structures for the marketing team, we realized that some of their problems were actually company wide.

There were daily standups, sprint meetings, all-hands and town halls, one-on-ones, quarterly reporting, and weekly leadership—even a Friday night show-and-tell. And all of this was in addition to client, vendor, and other external meetings.

The CEO and most of the leadership team had calendars that were double- and triple-booked in fifteen-minute increments. It was madness. And it wasn't like these meetings were with clients to cocreate or learn from or with high-value prospects! The first thing we needed to do was review the cadence and structure as well as the rationale of all these meetings, eliminating them where we could, combining some, and reorganizing the rest into a more reasonable cadence to refocus energy toward impact.

Don't get me wrong: None of these meetings were "bad." There were just too many of them, and they weren't enabling flow or outcomes. They needed more structure around planning, cadence, and individual scheduling. They were actually interfering with the company's effectiveness rather than enhancing it. Restructuring these meetings freed the team to focus on the work and gave the executive team more flexibility to tackle the things that would allow the company to flourish.

The type and frequency of scheduled meetings are always driven by the size and type of your organization. If I had one piece of advice for every organization, it would be this: Don't adopt a meeting style and cadence just because it works for someone else or simply in the name of transparency. I've seen too many companies adopt or keep the whole team on daily standups as they scale instead of adjusting for the most efficient information flow between teams. If a daily meeting doesn't work for your team or your organization, don't do it. Find the style and cadence that works for your team, and focus on the results, not the format you use. Don't schedule a meeting just to have a meeting or to stick to an arbitrary schedule.

Structuring Meetings

Meetings, as the pandemic has proven, should be carefully thought out and structured so that each serves a specific purpose and maximizes communication and engagement with your team. You want to focus on getting the best ideas from your people and creating a sense of purpose and belonging.

Collecting and documenting information is also a must-have in process. If you don't stay organized, you'll eventually run into a setback, slowing down what could have otherwise been a productive work process. But while I might easily say, "Write everything down," I would be dooming you to endlessly collect and blend useful and useless info.

While it is important to write down what is communicated and collect the appropriate information, the key word is *appropriate*. My team and I are now fully remote, and we've embraced a suite of tools that allow us to document and share the output of each of our meetings. For example, we use Otter.ai to create a transcript of internal meetings in addition to the usual recording for visuals or live whiteboard capture. As a result, we can trace the development and implementation of each of our ideas from genesis through fully executed product or service.

Experimentation

To quote Rear Admiral Grace Murray Hopper, "The most damaging phrase in the language is 'We've always done it this way!'"[4] Admiral Hopper really knew what she was talking about. In all my work, from the earliest-stage startups to giant legacy corporations, the inability to experiment with process is one of the major stumbling blocks to innovation.

Whenever an innovator asks me, "What's the best way to build an X process?" the initial response seems unsatisfactory: "It depends." That's usually followed by a series of questions: *What's the outcome you're looking for? What's your timeline? Who's building the process? Why do you need it? How many team members or collaborators will be involved? Who's responsible for managing it after it's built? Are there any entrenched tools in the tech stack that can't be eliminated?*

Annoying, right? One of the hardest things to do is change the mindset of people who believe in off-the-shelf, context-free solutions. Just because someone else has done it this way before doesn't mean it will work for you.

I'm not advocating for a free-for-all when it comes to process-building, but I am saying that it is itself an ongoing process. Of course, you need stable systems in place in order to have a functional organization. But process is not a one-and-done deal. Innovation requires that you periodically review not just what you're doing but how you're doing it.

One of my favorite techniques is building parallel safe-to-fail experiments. These are small experiments designed to allow new possibilities and opportunities to emerge. By running several small experiments at the same time, you can watch as the interactions they create affect your processes.[5]

In other words, we're not trying to destroy your system; we're introducing small changes to see what happens. If it fails, it's not catastrophic, and it's within the guardrails of what leadership deems as low-risk failure. But if it succeeds, we've discovered a possible innovation. It allows us to test different strategies and tactics while minimizing risk.

Failure Is Part of the Process

When you saw *failure* in the heading just now, you cringed a little, right? Join the club, my friend. We have been indoctrinated to fear failure from our earliest years. Our parents often set us up with the pretense that failure is bad. It's the basis of our educational system. It's an integral part of corporate life. It's where impostor syndrome often stems from. It's one of the worst things you can say to someone: "You are such a failure."

Well, it's time to get over that. That mindset is the antithesis of what a startup is all about. Failure is part of everything we do. The only way to succeed at something is to do it wrong until you figure out how to do it right; that's learning. Sometimes things work, and sometimes they don't. But fear of failure is one of the biggest blocks to innovative thinking. When

If you want to create a process that encourages innovation, you must make failure a part of your company culture.

we get caught in the thinking–feeling loop, it can block our ability to take action, especially inspired action.

If you want to create a process that encourages innovation, you must make failure a part of your company culture. You need to abandon the idea that failure is punished. A mistake should be a learning experience, not a career death sentence.

A 2020 McKinsey article laid out four key principles for creating an environment where it's safe to fail:[6]

- The CEO has the key role in creating an environment where people understand they won't be punished for failing.
- Companies need to set certain safety nets in order to cultivate a comfortable enough environment where people are willing to take risks and make bold decisions.
- Technology is making failure more acceptable.
- A willingness to fail must be embedded in a company's culture.

So, Lauren, how do you deal with failure? I hear you, and it's been a journey. I, too, have been guilty of chasing perfection. I've worked hard to accept that uncertainty and failure are part of every process.

And I count it as one of my greatest strengths. But it has not always been easy, and sometimes I had to learn the hard way.

My first true startup growth experience was with a founder I'll call Matt. Matt had heard about me through word of mouth and contacted me to discuss scaling his startup venture. He tried to convince me to go in-house to drive company growth and build out his marketing process. I hesitated but finally accepted. It was truly too good an opportunity to pass up.

So Matt and I dove in, and things went so well that the company's revenue very quickly grew exponentially. My team and I were building a marketing process that I believed was efficient, effective, and scalable. I was over the moon, and so was he.

But then, in the middle of all that success, I found that I had made an error in judgment on a paid search program. I prematurely launched a campaign that hadn't been properly firetested before putting a significant budget behind it. It ended up costing a substantial amount of money. It wasn't a catastrophic mistake—very expensive but, thankfully, not fatal—but I hesitated to tell Matt. I was young and inexperienced enough to believe that only perfection was acceptable.

When I finally confessed, I got one of the biggest surprises of my life: Matt simply looked at me and asked, "If you're not making mistakes, you're not taking enough risk. So, what did you learn?"

It took me a moment, but then I described what I had learned from the mistake and how I would adapt the decision-making and testing process going forward.

Matt gave me advice that I have carried with me throughout my career: "Why would I fire you now? You've made a mistake, and now you'll know exactly how to prevent them in the future. I fully expected you—and people in general—to make mistakes. It's how we choose to handle and learn from them that helps us move forward. I only ask that someone be able to recognize failures, apply them, and then try to monetize them." The faster you can fail and turn those failures into insights and apply them to your process, the faster the company can grow and learn alongside its people.

Because of that early experience, I've tried to look for ways for my own employees and team members to address their fear of failure. Creating an environment of trust and innovation is not easy, but it is also very rewarding. I love coaching people to their best performance. You'll find it takes time to learn how to coach your team members to treat mistakes or failures as learning experiences, but that time is well spent. I make it clear to any team I'm a part of that we're all there to learn, not criticize, and that learning happens through positive reinforcement. Growth comes from tension. Much like athletic training, we have to push our edge to grow. And the only real failure is a failure to learn and grow.

Scalability

Scale is critical to most commercial efforts. Every founder and innovator needs to think about how their product or service—and the process that brings them from concept to delivery—will grow over time.

Scale is a tricky subject. It's one of those things that depends on what you, the entrepreneur or innovator, are trying to achieve. Do you want to quickly sell when you reach a certain size? Do you want a company you run for your entire career? What are your company's expectations of innovation? These are all questions that affect your approach to scaling. Building the right kind of processes and systems is critical to any efforts at scale. It's easy to fall into the trap of thinking that the processes that got you to $1 million in sales will get you to $10 million or $100 million and beyond.

There's always a moment for leaders when they realize they don't know the names of everyone who works for them or that they no longer have a personal relationship with each and every customer. That is the moment when you realize the importance of the processes you've built. By creating a critical infrastructure that reflects your values, you can be sure that those new employees understand what they have to do and why they have to do it. And the customers who you don't know understand that you prize delivering value above all else.

Once you have all your processes and systems in place, your leadership needs to focus on the balance between a stable base and an agile response. This seems overwhelming, I'll admit, but I promise you'll be just fine.

Several years ago, at a conference, I met a founder whose company had moved beyond the startup stage to become a successful business. He told me that one of his most profound entrepreneurial experiences was the first morning he walked down the office hallway and passed two people he didn't recognize. They were clearly employees, but for the first time, he didn't remember their names or hiring them. That was an aha moment, when he realized he needed to make sure that, even if he didn't know everyone's name, there was someone whose job it was to know how to find out everyone's name. It gave him a real appreciation for how important it is to have a talent acquisition process that accurately reflects the company's mission and values.

And Finally . . .

Process is one of the places where the value of thinking like a brand and acting like a startup is crystal clear. When you're developing processes, whether in the smallest startup or a corporate innovation lab, the balance between stability and agility is key to that development. As one of my heroes, Steve Blank, has said, "Processes reduce risk to an overall organization, but each layer of process reduces the ability to be agile and lean and—most importantly—responsive to new opportunities and threats."[7]

One of the biggest mistakes many ventures, big and small, make is trying to adopt the processes of successful companies wholesale. For example, you might hear, "We run everything just like Steve Jobs did." But they're not Steve Jobs, so that process may not work for them. You can't copy and paste someone else's process and hope for the best. Also, good process isn't easy to implement and execute; it takes commitment and investment. Be sure to experiment as much as possible early on to find what works for you.

Process isn't sexy (well, it is for me), but it is always necessary. And once you start getting attracted to a lack of waste, you'll develop the same love for process I have. So start working on that today. You'll thank me later.

Kevin at Big Brand

The innovation team is discussing how their internal processes will integrate into Big Brand's existing processes and infrastructure.

"If we mirror the existing process architecture in ours, it will smooth the handoffs," Kevin begins.

Tiff raises her hand. "Kev, we've been wondering if just mirroring our current processes is the right way to go. We know we can't mess with budgeting, HR, all that, but ..."

continued

"I don't see how to avoid it," Kevin replies. "We work for Big Brand, and they're expecting results they can use."

"I know, but can we really innovate by doing the same old things? Aria was talking about something really interesting the other day that might help us."

"Thanks for putting me on the spot, Tiff." Aria is clearly a little nervous about addressing the whole group. "A speaker at the South Summit conference last year was talking about safe-to-fail experiments.[8] I asked some follow-up questions, and we talked about how safe-to-fail experiments allow you to observe how changes affect your system without disrupting the entire thing."

"That actually sounds interesting," Kevin says. "What's involved?"

Aria says, "Think about how structured Big Brand's processes are; it runs on a very rule-based, context-free, best-practice system. We are in a different space trying to build something new that needs to interact with Big Brand's process without causing a massive failure. Our processes need to be more emergent based on the context."

"Okay, I'm with you," Kevin says.

Aria chugs her coffee. "Safe-to-fail experiments could help us build processes that will achieve our outcomes and minimize the risk to the overall system. Running parallel safe-to-fail experiments is like placing several small bets simultaneously to hedge your risk. The trick is to have a good hypothesis to inform your bets."

"I don't think I can sell failure to the executive team,"

Kevin says. "They really only like to talk about how we're going to succeed."

"A McKinsey article talks about the importance of quantifying failure not just as the potential loss but also the potential gains and the lost opportunity cost.[9] Big Brand's systems work really well for a commodities company, but we're trying to move the company forward. Those are not the same thing. We have to make the potential for failure a normal part of doing business for this team."

Tiff says, "Big Brand is expecting an inherently risky undertaking to be risk averse. It doesn't add up."

"Right," Aria explains. "We're trying to mitigate the risk while experimenting with different ways to achieve our outcomes. Let's try it out."

They get to work. By the end of the day, the entire team has settled on two promising hypotheses and addressed a few of the questions for several potential experiments. They've decided to have two different working groups to produce two different safe-to-fail experiments that will run for a pre-determined length of time.

Kevin is so pleased he sends Aria a box of chocolates.

Within a few months, the team has determined several new ways to approach a process that doesn't go against Big Brand's guidelines but encourages the process of innovation. In one case, their experiment convinced Big Brand teams to make small changes to their processes to increase efficiency and effectiveness.

Meg wants to talk bonus with Kevin.

continued

"The team is staging a mini revolt," Jamal says in a lunch meeting with Sarah and Alex.

"Oh, it's not that bad," Sarah interjects. "They are just saying they need more guidance. The other day Nik said we need more structure."

"Well, how are you going to address that?" Alex asks.

Jamal says, "They're always complaining."

Alex says, "I think Nik and your team are feeling untethered because you two are still managing reactively."

"Say more," Sarah replies.

"Every day you're putting out fires. But as a result, you treat everything like a fire drill: problem solved, next; problem solved, next. Your team never knows how their work affects the decision-making process—or if there even is one."

"Of course we have a decision-making process," Jamal interjects. "We know what needs to be done, and Sarah and I work together to make the right decisions."

Alex says, "You know the problem that's right in front of you, but do you know if you have the right information to make a decision? Do you know how the decision will affect the other systems in your company? Does the team understand why the decision was made? You're not really making decisions at the moment; you're simply reacting. Your company can't scale if your people and systems don't have a way to grow as well."

"We have to grow and become self-sufficient," Jamal says. "Our investors are tired of cash infusions."

"A system that works with a small team like yours won't work with a larger team. Neither will your current decision-making process. You'll never be able to keep up."

"So how do we start thinking about scaling when we're still trying to get through next week?" Sarah asks.

"Here's a quick exercise that will help you understand where startups frequently fail. I'll email it to you, but I'll draw it on a napkin for now.

"McKinsey's four quadrants help you understand the current state of your system.[10] Ideally, you want to have your team fill it out individually. Everyone wants to be in the *strong agile* section, but you'll probably find yourself under *startup* instead. The point isn't to check all the boxes in your favorite quadrant; it's to find the balance that you need to grow your company."

"More homework," Jamal groans.

"But he's right," Sarah says. "We are just living in the moment instead of keeping our eye on the future as well."

"Okay, we'll give it a shot," Jamal says. "Alex, I don't know whether to thank you or throw something at you."

Three weeks later Sarah and Jamal invite Alex to lunch again.

"Well?" Alex asks after they order. "What did you find out from the quadrant exercise?"

"I felt like I got hit by a truck," Sarah replies. "We didn't realize how worried the team was about our decision-making."

Alex nods. "They just needed a way to let you know how the lack of stability was affecting them. You were trying to be agile because speed seems essential. But the trick is to find a

continued

balance between stability and agility. You do that by building fast feedback loops so your team can get you the right information and you can let them know how you are making a decision. That allows the team to see how information flows through the loop.

"Building the right process is an ongoing process itself. You'll face a new context and set of challenges at every stage of your growth. By building a resilient system that balances stability and agility, you should be ready for anything."

Chapter 10

The Future

I t should be clear by now that I believe the key to any successful endeavor, from the earliest-stage startup to the largest venture or innovation lab, is leveraging the duality of stability and agility. I'm well aware that I'm repeating myself, but repetition is often the best way to make an idea stick. This is why I've been advising founders and innovators to think like a brand and act like a startup for more than a decade. Let's take a moment to recap.

Startups are renowned for their agility, characterized by fast decision-making, on-the-fly experimentation, and a willingness to take risks. These qualities often enable them to scale rapidly and achieve remarkable growth. However, once the initial momentum fades, their lack of focus on establishing stable, repeatable processes, structures, and pipelines shoots them in the foot. They are super agile, but, too often, they can't really scale that agility. Consistency is the secret to scale.

Big brands, on the other hand, really know how to scale. They are filled with those stable, repeatable processes and pipelines I just mentioned. Mega corps like Microsoft build for scale from the beginning, even in their startup division. But they're not as adept at being first to market with the newest and latest innovations. If there's something I've observed from working at Microsoft and Nike, though, it is their ability to build and consistently monetize their cultlike brand consistency. The stability that enables them to capture market share makes it difficult for them to nurture the small ideas that have a chance to grow into the next big thing.

Yet Nike and Microsoft are two large corporations that have had more innovation success than many. For instance, NIKE created an innovation lab and digital products while Microsoft turned to startup acquisitions like GitHub, LinkedIn, and joint venture partnerships like Open AI to harness startup agility outside of their core business. But the large size and structure of most large corporations are still ultimately slowing them down, with Nike losing market share to up and comers like Hoka and others. However, the stability of the larger corporations also provides a really strong strategic foundation, which allows them to understand their role in the competitive market and supports ongoing product–market fit. Their decision-making and workflows are often not built for fail-fast or safe-to-fail experimentation. They tend to think in terms of features or product portfolios. Unfortunately, this leaves them open to unexpected competition from hungry, fast-moving startups.

By bringing the best of both worlds, cutting what doesn't work, and learning how to be stable yet agile at the same time, innovators like you can build ventures that have the best chance for sustainable success. This mindset and way of leading will become your Trojan horse.

What does the future hold for our heroes?

You've seen our intrepid explorers struggle to find the balance between stability and agility in the persona stories: Kevin is trying to introduce agility into an extremely stable environment of products, processes, and leadership functions. While Sarah and Jamal are under both internal and external pressure to stabilize their company's operations.

In Kevin's case, there are four possibilities for the future of his endeavor:

- His team is responsible for a game-changing innovation, and his lab is funded indefinitely.

- No matter how successful his team is, during the next economic downturn, his funding disappears, and Big Brand offers him a lateral move or a promotion for being a good employee.

- He gets poached by another brand to build a hybrid venture studio, leveraging his learnings and the emerging business and funding model.

- He meets one or more aspiring innovators interested in the same things with access to capital and networks to found a new venture.

If I was a betting woman, I'd guess that the second scenario is the most likely. One of the unfortunate side effects of the stability of most big brands is that they are at the mercy of the financial markets and quarterly earnings reports. So when the economy slumps and the bottom line suffers, innovation is often the first thing to go. This short-term, market-based thinking is slowly changing, but the pace of that change is glacial.

Regardless of what Big Brand does, Kevin will be fine. His journey is about developing the two most important skills in a leader's toolbox: listening and adapting. No matter which of the four options unfold, these qualities will allow Kevin to shine.

Sarah and Jamal's future is less clear. A lot depends on whether or not they learn to communicate effectively with their team and stakeholders about every aspect of the company. The paths I see for these two are these:

- Their investors lose confidence, they run out of funding, and they are forced to close shop.

- Their innovative product launches and takes the market by storm, and they are acquired by a larger entity.

- The board forces a sale to the highest bidder or sells off the IP.

- They focus all their resources on prioritizing pipeline to build traction and a sustainable venture.

Sarah and Jamal want option four, assuming they have a choice. They love their team, they love building a company and community, and they want to grow and scale into a major player in their industry. The potential is there, but scaling means they need to leave some of the startup chaos behind. Embracing experimentation and flexibility while creating and building a flexible, stable process that supports flow and momentum for brand, product, and community building is one of the biggest components of scalability.

We've seen them struggle with clearly sharing their strategies and plans as things change. They have trouble communicating with every level of their company: their team, the stakeholders, and even with each other. Communication and trust between the stakeholders are make-or-break factors of the company and launch. If they succeed and go beyond expectations by easing the communication and overall flow, option four becomes more realistic. If they fail to achieve better communication and just hope it works out, they'll find that their options are limited.

These stories are about people trying to create innovative products and services in very different environments. Kevin is trying to build a disparate group of people from different departments of a giant corporation into an effective innovation team. His story is really about learning from those around him about what works and what doesn't in his specific situation. And the same is true of Sarah and Jamal; they had a lot of theories about what would build an effective organization, but they were forced to learn from all their different stakeholders about the gaps between theory and practice.

What Kevin, Sarah, and Jamal have in common is the need to build a community that fosters a culture of success and well-being. None of them can succeed with a group of alienated, exhausted, angry stakeholders. They need to find a way to meet the challenges that come with creating a cohesive community focused on a successful, sustainable, scalable future. The future of work will depend on a combination of work, talent, and well-being for both the workforce and leadership. If we put in processes, support, and a mindset for taking care of our people, they'll take care of the business in turn. How do we get to that stage? Well, it's a process.

Takeaways

Those are some of the future possibilities that are available to Kevin, Sarah, and Jamal. Now let's talk about you. We've covered a lot of things you should think about, look for, and do—but it's a lot. So here are the three key points I want you to take away from this book:

The Tools

I've referenced different techniques and tools that I use to help founders and innovators create dynamic work and communication flows. I'm always cautious about recommending particular ones. Many of you will be constrained by cost, time, team preferences, and differences in leadership or may need to use what your company already has available. And that's okay. The important things about thinking like a brand and acting like a startup are less about what you use and more about how you use them. Always keep in mind that the most important concept is correctly identifying the goal or problem before you try to find a solution.

Even the stories of Kevin, Sarah, and Jamal are the product of one of these tools: persona mapping, originally a marketing tool that is now used throughout organizations to create more customer-centric products and services. These techniques are starting to take on larger roles within the corporate, entrepreneurial, and innovation ecosystems, especially as founders and corporate trailblazers seek new ways to improve their business outcomes and scale new ventures.

Design-thinking tools, like persona mapping and the Business Model Canvas, are incredibly useful. These tools, and others like them, help us manage our day-to-day work and personal lives, but they're just the tip of the iceberg. The development of artificial intelligence systems will foster explosive growth in collaboration within and among industry, brands, startups, academia, and the public sector. And recent events like the global pandemic have highlighted the need for that kind of broad collaboration and consensus.

For over a decade I have been saying that the ability to leverage more diverse resources across big brands, startups, venture capital, and even in public sectors is where the real value is generated. These added tools and diversification of value-creation will fuel productivity, something all companies aspire to increase. People will be faced with new learnings and explorations, a crucial element of increasing motivation to work and be productive. With the acceleration COVID-19 brought, and the disruption of AI, the world is more than ready to pivot to new forms of value-creation and increase productivity in the workplace.

Going back to the core of what this book is all about, agility is your willingness to adopt and try new tech, tools, experimentation methods, and emerging AI. Stability is how well you can then integrate these new innovations and scale with them, ensuring they work seamlessly with your existing operations, old and new strategies, and the perspectives of everyone involved.

The People

Obviously, I think tools are great. I've spent a large part of my career in the tech space, and I've reveled in being an early adopter of all kinds of tech. But if you've been paying attention, you'll have noticed that this book is really about people.

Everything is built around people—whether it's your team, other stakeholders, or customers. The human touch is crucial to the organization from how their interactions configure processes; how their insights, hard work, and commitment contribute to every company, regardless of size; and how much they have to teach their leaders about everything from product design to leadership.

Technology has always introduced disruption into existing systems. Personal computers, smartphones,

Everything is built around people.

and even typewriters, telephones, and automobiles caused profound disruption to existing industries and social structures. But there were humans standing behind each new innovation, contributing to the astounding progress we see all around us today. Even as the world becomes more tech- and AI-driven, humans are going to become even more crucial to supporting the systems, ethics, and underlying processes that are needed to keep them running smoothly.

The Learning

The most effective way to learn is through failure. There, I said the scary part out loud, and I doubt you haven't heard it before. One of the biggest problems I faced in my business career was the inability and unwillingness to address failure. Sure, some individual entrepreneurs and innovators can embrace and learn from failures, but the vast majority of us remain extremely risk averse. And that's too bad. I've seen lots of lost opportunities because the downside was too intimidating.

We've discussed a lot of examples of failure, but the point of these stories is not the failures themselves but the recovery. The balance of stability and agility (yes, yes, I keep talking about it) is what allows an organization or even a person to use what they learn to succeed in their next venture. Learning is not just about taking a course, reading a book, or watching a webinar; it's about trying things out, figuring out what ideas work, leaving behind the ones that don't, and moving on. You don't want to try something that will destroy the organization, of course, but you do want to create a controlled environment where you can measure the effects of your ideas. It's not just asking whether things improved; it's also asking how much improvement you saw, whether it is repeatable, and whether it is scalable.

I like this quote from a *Wired* article. It's about scientists, but it captures the mistake that most people make when trying to experiment.

> Very infrequently do you get a science process story, one where a scientist will lay out all the ways an experiment failed, and failed again, and failed again . . . If you're reading a news story about science, it's almost always about the successes—the breakthroughs, the cures, the mysteries solved.[1]

The article goes on to talk about studies that show that resilience and high failure tolerance are critical for people staying in science. These two skills are also essential for any founder or innovator and both the cultures and ventures they foster. They're what allow you to continually probe your environment and find the right path forward or the next pivot.

Don't forget that this learning is continuous. If you're not upgrading your skills and knowledge, you're in trouble. I don't mean going back to school for an advanced degree, although you might. I'm talking about continually finding new information, tools, or skills that allow you to respond to the changes in environment or circumstance that you have no control over. This is the basis of the agility that I've been going on and on about: knowledge and information. It is important to be constantly learning, and it doesn't all have to be on you. The most successful entrepreneurs and leaders I know surround themselves with people who they can learn from so that everyone grows together.

As I write this, the world is abuzz with talk of the new generative AI and machine-learning models that promise to automate more and more tasks. Am I an expert in AI? No. But am I making it my business to learn at least enough to know what its impact will be on me and those who come to me seeking advice? You betcha!

The pace of change is increasing and the impact of those changes in the long and short term is becoming harder to predict. So, for me, learning as much as I can about each change, good and bad, is what's necessary for any business to survive and thrive.

And Finally . . . (I mean it this time)

One of the biggest myths and the hardest to overcome in the startup new venture world is that it's all struggle and grind in the short term for a big payout at the end. That's not how it works for most of us. Don't get me wrong; the struggle is real and failing is never fun. Instead, I suggest taking a more experimental approach, with clear breaks in the process to assess and decide to reinvest, retest, or pivot. In doing this, you can minimize the cost, related stress, and weight of that failure to arm yourself with the tools that allow you to succeed next time. It's not about viewing the grind as a badge of honor. These tools and learnings provide a sustained, creative approach to the problems you're presented with. Embracing those tools with a sense of optimism and openness lets us see the brilliant future before us.

The ultimate goal is to drive growth and innovation by harnessing the complementary nature of brand stability and startup agility. What started as a hypothesis a decade ago has turned into a core belief that the future doesn't have to be entirely random, but can be designed—and it will be built by those who can think like a brand and act like a startup.

Notes

Chapter 1

1. BBVA, "Latin America's Roadmap to Innovation: The Most Enterprising Cities," BBVA Open Innovation, October 11, 2022, https://www.bbva.com/en/latin-americas-roadmap-to -innovation-the-most-enterprising-cities.

2. Mariana Costa Checa (founder, Laboratoria), interview with the author through WhatsApp, October 8, 2022.

3. Costa Checa, interview.

4. *MIT Technology Review*, "Mariana Costa," Innovators under 35, 2015, https://www.innovatorsunder35.com/the-list/ mariana-costa.

5. Abraham Taipe, "Mark Zuckerberg: Un emprendimiento peruano como ejemplo mundial," *El Comercio*, November 19, 2016, https://elcomercio.pe/economia/mark-zuckerberg-emprendimiento-peruano-ejemplo-mundial-432313-noticia/#google_vignette.

6. "Mariana Costa Checa," Wikipedia, August 20, 2023, https://en.wikipedia.org/wiki/Mariana_Costa_Checa.

7. Laboratoria Staff, "What Is Laboratoria?" Laboratoria, September 19, 2022, https://hub.laboratoria.la/en/laboratoria.

8. Costa Checa, interview.

9. Workhuman, "Unleashing the Human Element at Work: Transforming Workplaces through Recognition," May 11, 2022, https://www.workhuman.com/resources/reports-guides/unleashing-the-human-element-at-work-transforming-workplaces-through-recognition/.

10. CB Insights, https://www.cbinsights.com.

11. Bailey Reiners, "21 Company Culture Examples to Get You Inspired," Built In, March 29, 2023, https://builtin.com/company-culture/company-culture-examples.

12. Costa Checa, interview.

13. Aaron De Smet, Gregor Jost, and Leigh Weiss, "Three Keys to Faster, Better Decisions," *McKinsey Quarterly*, McKinsey & Company, May 1, 2019, https://www.mckinsey.com/capabilities/people-and-organizational-performance/our-insights/three-keys-to-faster-better-decisions.

14. "Golden Circle for Organizations," The Optimism Company from Simon Sinek, https://simonsinek.com/product/golden-circle-for-organizations/.

15. Simon Sinek, "The Infinite Game," *New York Times* Events, May 31, 2018, YouTube video, https://www.youtube.com/watch?v=tye525dkfi8.

Chapter 2

1. "USS *John S. McCain* and *Alnic MC* collision," Wikipedia, August 6, 2023, https://en.wikipedia.org/wiki/USS_John_S._McCain_and_Alnic_MC_collision.

2. Omar Ibn Abdillah, "10 Differences between Startups and Small Businesses," LinkedIn, December 5, 2022, https://www.linkedin.com/pulse/10-differences-between-startups-small-businesses-omar-ibn-abdillah.

3. Simon Sinek, *Start with Why: How Great Leaders Inspire Everyone to Take Action* (New York: Penguin, 2009).

4. KPI.org, "What Is a Key Performance Indicator (KPI)?" 2023, https://kpi.org/KPI-Basics.

5. Eric Andrews, "Spotify Doesn't Use OKRs Anymore . . . Should You?" *Medium*, January 21, 2020, https://medium.com/@ericandrews603/spotify-doesnt-use-okrs-anymore-should-you-3927eeaa22dd.

6. Farrah Smith, "The Top 5 Habits of Peak Performing Entrepreneurs," *Entrepreneur*, May 3, 2021, https://www.entrepreneur.com/leadership/the-top-5-habits-of-peak-performing-entrepreneurs/367310.

Chapter 3

1. Kate Leggett, "Customer Service: Why It Matters—and How to Do It Right," Forrester, January 4, 2013, https://www.forrester.com/blogs/13-01-04-customer_service_why_it_matters_and_how_to_do_it_right/#:~:text=Customer%20satisfaction%20correlates%20to%20customer,customer%20service%20experiences%20are%20expensive.

2. Niklas Stattin, "32 Customer Experience Statistics You Need to Know for 2024," SuperOffice, September 1, 2023, https://www.superoffice.com/blog/customer-experience-statistics.

3. Grand View Research, *Movies and Entertainment Market Size, Share and Trends Analysis Report by Product (Movies, Music, and Videos), by Region, and Segment Forecasts, 2022–2030*, 2021, https://www.grandviewresearch.com/industry-analysis/movies-entertainment-market.

4. Fortune Business Insights, *Video Streaming Market Size, Share & COVID-19 Impact Analysis, by Component (Software and Content Delivery Services), by Channel (Satellite TV, Cable TV, Internet Protocol Television (IPTV), and OTT Streaming), by Vertical (Education/E-Learning, Healthcare, Government, Sports/eSports, Gaming, Enterprise and Corporate, Auction and Bidding, Fitness & Lifestyle, Music & Entertainment, and Others (Transportation)), and Regional Forecast, 2023–2030*, May 2023, https://www.fortunebusinessinsights.com/video-streaming-market-103057.

5. Accenture Interactive, "Personalization Pulse Check 2018: Making It Personal," Infographic, 2018, https://www.accenture.com/_acnmedia/pdf-83/accenture-pulse-check-infographic.pdf.

6. Stuart R. Levine, "Diversity Confirmed to Boost Innovation and Financial Results," *Forbes*, January 15, 2020, https://www.forbes.com/sites/forbesinsights/2020/01/15/diversity-confirmed-to-boost-innovation-and-financial-results.

7. Statista Research Department, "Value of Venture Capital Funding to Female-Only and Male/Female Cofounded Startups Worldwide between 2011 and 2020 (in Billion U.S. Dollars)," Statista, January 11, 2022, https://www.statista.com/statistics/1221702/value-global-venture-capital-funding-to-startups-by-gender.

8. Fredrik Hanell, "Why Are There Not More Female Co-founders in Startups?" EIT Urban Mobility, March 8, 2021, https://www.eiturbanmobility.eu/why-are-there-not-more-female-co-founders-in-startups.

9.   Emma Bakh, "How to Bridge the Customer Expectation Gap," FullView, 2023, https://www.fullview.io/blog/how-to-bridge-the-customer-expectation-gap.

10. David J. Bland, "How Assumptions Mapping Can Focus Your Teams on Running Experiments that Matter," Strategyzer, August 4, 2020, https://www.strategyzer.com/blog/how-assumptions-mapping-can-focus-your-teams-on-running-experiments-that-matter.

11. David J. Bland, "Precoil: How to Get Started with Assumptions Mapping," September 6, 2016, YouTube video, https://www.youtube.com/watch?v=PyCvsBrKO4w.

12. James Allen, Frederick F. Reichheld, and Barney Hamilton, "The Three 'Ds' of Customer Experience," *Working Knowledge*, Harvard Business School, November 7, 2005, https://hbswk.hbs.edu/archive/the-three-ds-of-customer-experience.

Chapter 4

1.   Clayton M. Christensen, *The Innovator's Dilemma: When New Technologies Cause Great Firms to Fail* (Boston: Harvard Business Review Press, 1997).

2.   Alan Klement, "What Is Jobs to Be Done (JTBD)?" *Medium*, October 9, 2016, https://jtbd.info/2-what-is-jobs-to-be-done-jtbd-796b82081cca.

3.   Rob LaFranco and Chase Peterson-Withorn, eds., "The Richest in 2023," World's Billionaires List, *Forbes*, 2023, https://www.forbes.com/billionaires.

4.   Kristen Baker, "Customer Segmentation: How to Segment Users & Clients Effectively," HubSpot, May 24, 2023, https://blog.hubspot.com/service/customer-segmentation.

5.   General Assembly, "Who We Are," 2023, https://generalassemb.ly.

Chapter 5

1. Headspace, "About Headspace," 2023, https://www.headspace.com.

2. Metalab, "Mindfulness for Your Everyday Life," Metalab, 2023, https://www.metalab.com/projects/headspace.

3. Tom Whatley, "How Headspace Built a Content Marketing Strategy That Generates over 722,000 Monthly Organic Visitors," Grizzle, June 18, 2020, https://www.grizzle.io/blog/headspace.

4. Nigel Hollis, "Not Just Different but Meaningfully Different," *Millward Brown: Point of View*, Millward Brown, 2011, https://www.r-trends.ru/netcat_files/File/MillwardBrown_POV_Meaningfully_Different%20.pdf.

5. Seth Godin, "Define: Brand," Seth's Blog, December 13, 2009, https://seths.blog/2009/12/define-brand.

6. Julie Rice and Elizabeth Cutler, "SoulCycle | Julie Rice & Elizabeth Cutler | Talks at Google," Talks at Google, February 22, 2016, YouTube video, https://www.youtube.com/watch?v=6W25BydduZk.

7. Effy Pafitis, "Red Bull's Marketing Strategy: What Your Company Can Learn," Starting Business, January 28, 2020, https://www.startingbusiness.com/blog/marketing-strategy-red-bull.

8. AJ Agrawal, "Millennials Want Transparency and Social Impact. What Are You Doing to Build a Millennial-Friendly Brand?" *Entrepreneur*, May 31, 2018, https://www.entrepreneur.com/starting-a-business/millennials-want-transparency-and-social-impact-what-are/314156.

9. B Lab, "About B Corp Certification: Measuring a Company's Entire Social and Environmental Impact," 2023, https://www.bcorporation.net/en-us/certification.

10. I'm not talking about the Fourteenth Amendment and corporate personhood; that is another book, probably a heavy legal textbook.

11. Farhat Zishan, "A Closer Look at Nike's 'Dream Crazier' Campaign," BBF Digital, March 18, 2019, https://bbf.digital/nike-dream-crazier.

12. Claudia Wright, "Nike 'Dream Crazier' Ad: Empowering or Provoking?" The Dairy Agency, March 12, 2019, https://www.thedairyagency.co.uk/journal/nike-dream-crazier-ad-empowering-or-provoking.

13. Sam Levin, "Uber's Scandals, Blunders and PR Disasters: The Full List," *Guardian*, June 27, 2017, https://www.theguardian.com/technology/2017/jun/18/uber-travis-kalanick-scandal-pr-disaster-timeline.

14. Claire Lampen, "Bye Bye Mast Bros: Controversial Confectionary Hipsters Decamp for Mount Kisco," *Gothamist*, August 28, 2019, https://gothamist.com/food/bye-bye-mast-bros-confectionary-scammers-decamp-mount-kisco.

15. Maria Rosala, "Using 'How Might We' Questions to Ideate on the Right Problems," Nielsen Norman Group, January 17, 2021, https://www.nngroup.com/articles/how-might-we-questions.

Chapter 6

1. Grand View Research, *Meal Kit Delivery Services Market Size, Share & Trends Analysis Report by Offering (Heat & Eat, Cook & Eat), by Service (Single, Multiple), by Platform (Online, Offline), Meal Type (Vegan, Vegetarian), by Region, and Segment Forecasts, 2023–2030*, 2023, https://www.grandviewresearch.com/industry-analysis/meal-kit-delivery-services-market.

2. Al Ramadan, Dave Peterson, Christopher Lochhead, and Kevin Maney, *Play Bigger: How Pirates, Dreamers, and Innovators Create and Dominate Markets* (New York: HarperCollins, 2016), https://www.playbigger.com/book.

3. Daniel Kahneman, *Thinking, Fast and Slow* (New York: Farrar, Straus, and Giroux, 2013).

4. Strategyzer, "The Business Model Canvas," 2020, https://www .strategyzer.com/canvas/business-model-canvas.

5. https://www.crunchplus.com.

6. David Curry, "Peloton Revenue and Usage Statistics (2023)," Business of Apps, August 16, 2023, https://www .businessofapps.com/data/peloton-statistics.

7. Jordan Crook, "With $2 Million in New Seed Funding, Classtivity Rebrands as ClassPass to Add Variety to Your Workout," *TechCrunch+*, March 31, 2014, http://tcrn. ch/1hrBp0i.

8. Dan Primack, "Mindbody Acquires ClassPass, Merger Gets $500 Million Investment," *Axios*, October 14, 2021, https://www.axios. com/2021/10/14/midbody-buys-classpass-merger-investment.

Chapter 7

1. Tarryn Giebelmann, "Why Business Flow Is Essential for Success," Sage, July 15, 2022, https://www.sage.com/en-za/blog/ why-business-flow-is-essential-for-success/#gate-84fe79b5 -668d-41f8-a0cc-6229018c4ac9.

2. The Team at Slack, "Practices for Managing Information Flows within Organizations," Slack, February 7, 2022, https:// slack.com/blog/collaboration/practices-for-managing -information-flows.

3. Hansani Bandara, "How to Build a Passive Talent Pipeline in 4 Steps," Creately, October 19, 2022, https://creately.com/blog/business/how-to-build-a-talent-pipeline.

4. Forbes Technology Council, "13 Reasons Google Deserves Its 'Best Company Culture' Award," *Forbes*, February 8, 2018, https://www.forbes.com/sites/forbestechcouncil/2018/02/08/13-reasons-google-deserves-its-best-company-culture-award.

5. Martin Luenendonk, "The Leadership Pipeline Model: Building the Next-Generation Leaders," Cleverism, July 25, 2020, https://www.cleverism.com/leadership-pipeline-model.

6. IDEO, "How to Prototype a New Business," IDEO U, 2023, https://www.ideou.com/blogs/inspiration/how-to-prototype-a-new-business.

Chapter 8

1. Bailey Reiners, "21 Company Culture Examples to Get You Inspired," Built In, March 28, 2023, https://builtin.com/company-culture/company-culture-examples.

2. Brian Nordli, "Careers That Tell a Story: How CB Insights Helps Its Employees Grow," Built In, May 30, 2018, https://www.builtinnyc.com/2018/05/30/CB-Insights-Culture-Spotlight.

3. Emma Seppälä and Kim Cameron, "Proof that Positive Work Cultures Are More Productive," *Harvard Business Review*, December 1, 2015, https://hbr.org/2015/12/proof-that-positive-work-cultures-are-more-productive.

4. Lennart Pedersen, "Evidence Shows That Positive Work Cultures Are More Productive," LinkedIn, December 28, 2015, https://www.linkedin.com/pulse/evidence-shows-positive-work-cultures-more-productive-pedersen.

5. Alex Ward, "The Sixth Man," *New York Times Magazine*, March 4, 1984, https://www.nytimes.com/1984/03/04/magazine/the-sixth-man.html.

6. Chris Riches, "The Invaluable Sixth Man," Functional Basketball Coaching, February 22, 2013, https://functionalbasketballcoaching.com/the-invaluable-sixth-man.

7. Rob Cross, Reb Rebele, and Adam Grant, "Collaborative Overload," *Harvard Business Review*, January–February 2016, https://hbr.org/2016/01/collaborative-overload.

8. Paul Glatzhofer, "Past Behavior Is the Best Predictor of Future Behavior," Talogy, 2023, https://www.talogy.com/en/blog/past-behavior-is-the-best-predictor-of-future-behavior.

9. Shane Snow, *Dream Teams: Working Together Without Falling Apart* (New York: Portfolio/Penguin, 2018).

10. Marcus Buckingham and Gallup Organization, *First, Break All the Rules: What the World's Greatest Managers Do Differently* (New York: Simon & Schuster, 1999).

Chapter 9

1. DocuSign, "Kayak Says Bon Voyage to Paper-Based Processes," 2023, https://www.docusign.co.uk/customer-stories/kayak.

2. Brendan Morrow, "Big changes are coming for Netflix. Here's what to expect," *Yahoo! News*, April 29, 2022, https://news.yahoo.com/big-changes-coming-netflix-heres-095210805.html.

3. Steven MacDonald, "How to Create a Customer-Centric Strategy for Your Business," SuperOffice, February 21, 2023, https://www.superoffice.com/blog/how-to-create-a-customer-centric-strategy.

4. Esther Surden, "Privacy Laws May Usher in 'Defensive DP': Hopper," *Computerworld*, January 26, 1976.

5. David Gurteen, "Safe-to-Fail Experiments," *Conversational Leadership*, 2023, https://conversational-leadership.net/safe-to -fail-experiments.

6. McKinsey & Company, "Have You Made It Safe to Fail?" February 18, 2020, https://www.mckinsey.com/capabilities/ mckinsey-digital/our-insights/fasttimes/have-you-made-it -safe-to-fail.

7. Steve Blank, "Why Companies Do 'Innovation Theater' Instead of Actual Innovation," *Harvard Business Review*, October 7, 2019, https://hbr.org/2019/10/why-companies-do-innovation -theater-instead-of-actual-innovation.

8. South Summit Conference, https://www.southsummit.co.

9. Laura DeLallo, "Building Data-Driven Culture: An Interview with ShopRunner CEO Sam Yagan," *McKinsey Quarterly*, McKinsey & Company, February 14, 2019, https://www .mckinsey.com/capabilities/quantumblack/our-insights/ building-an-innovative-data-driven-culture-an-interview-with -shoprunner-ceo-sam-yagan.

10. Wouter Aghina, Aaron De Smet, and Kirsten Weerda, "Agility: It Rhymes with Stability," *McKinsey Quarterly*, McKinsey & Company, December 1, 2015, https://www.mckinsey.com/ capabilities/people-and-organizational-performance/our -insights/agility-it-rhymes-with-stability.

Chapter 10

1. Emily Dreyfuss, "Scientists Need to Talk More about Failure," *WIRED*, 25 April 25, 2019, https://www.wired.com/story/ scientists-need-more-failure-talk.

Index